GOLDRATT'S
RULES OF
FLOW

GOLDRATT'S
RULES OF
FLOW

EFRAT GOLDRATT-ASHLAG

Routledge
Taylor & Francis Group

LONDON AND NEW YORK

Illustrations by Chen Litman
Cover design by Addi Cohen-Ziv
Author photo by Roni Sofer

First published 2024
by Routledge
4 Park Square, Milton Park, Abingdon, Oxon OX14 4RN

and by Routledge
605 Third Avenue, New York, NY 10158

*Routledge is an imprint of the Taylor & Francis Group,
an informa business*

British Library Cataloguing-in-Publication Data
A catalogue record for this book is available from the British
Library

ISBN: 978-1-032-58006-7 (hbk)
ISBN: 978-1-032-57872-9 (pbk)

Typeset in Minion Pro
by North River Press

Printed and bound by CPI Group (UK) Ltd, Croydon, CR0 4YY

Contents

Contents

Improving flow is a primary objective of every operation.

Dr. Eli Goldratt
Standing on the Shoulders of Giants, 2008

Introduction

Dr. Eli Goldratt wrote his first book *The Goal*, to introduce his innovative thinking to improve operations.[1] The common belief, he claimed, is that if every machine is fully utilized, the entire operation will be efficient. Thus, managers attempt to maximize the efficiency of each and every machine and work center. That takes a lot of effort, but unfortunately it doesn't yield the desired results. Instead, managers should look at the whole operation, identify the bottlenecks and focus only on their productivity. He called it global optimum vs. local optimum. Written as an accessible business novel, *The Goal* became a worldwide best seller and is known as his introduction to Theory of Constraints (T.O.C.). Although a lot of the key concepts in the T.O.C. application for operations were developed later on, the fundamentals didn't change. In fact, *The Goal* is as relevant today as it was thirty-five years ago.

Project management is inherently different than production. For one, projects are not as repetitive as production. Every project is different and thus involve a lot more risk. Goldratt noticed that people working in projects make the same basic error: they manage the risk locally instead of looking at the whole picture. They tend to protect every activity, not the complete project, and the way they do it, the safety they incorporate is bound to be wasted. Goldratt called the new Theory of Constraints application CCPM (Critical Chain Project Management) and to introduce it he wrote another business novel, *Critical Chain*.[2] Originally, it included project planning and buffer management. The basic assumption in buffer management is simple: since projects are late because of unexpected delays, managers should use time buffers to protect against these delays. To protect the whole project, the main buffer should always be placed at the end of the project.

With more and more implementations around the world, CCPM proved itself as an excellent technique for managing projects. As the implementations started to accumulate, Goldratt noticed that in too many cases it wasn't as effective as it ought to be in shortening lead times. At first, he thought it was a matter of deciphering the details. A lot of effort was made by him, as well as many others, to figure out how to stagger tasks, where to place buffers, how to better calculate their size, et cetera. The results were pretty much the same. Goldratt started to suspect it wasn't about the details; the basic assumption was flawed. Before using buffers, the chaos in projects was so big that all people could do when things went wrong was point fingers at each other. But now, monitoring the buffers provided clarity that no one had before. Goldratt was able to examine the source of disruptions that consumed the buffers and what he found out was truly eye-opening. The time in projects was wasted not only by unexpected delays, but mainly by inherent obstacles that slow down the flow of projects. That was an astounding revelation. It was no longer about tweaking buffer management; it was about developing a new body of knowledge.

The years went by and Goldratt kept developing the Theory of Constraints and writing more books, while investigating the concept of flow. Whenever he got to talk about his books, he said that one day he'd replace *Critical Chain*; he'd rewrite it to introduce his new insights. In 2008 he wrote his article, "Standing on the Shoulders of Giants," to mark the 25th anniversary of *The Goal*.[3] This article discusses the origins of focusing on accelerating flow to improve performance in operations.

Around that same time, he released the strategic and tactical analysis of project management, his most comprehensive work on the subject. Although it was primarily about CCPM, the two major rules of flow—controlling WIP and full-kit already played a key role in it. People asked him if the time had finally come to rewrite *Critical Chain*. His answer was that he was busy writing another book, which he was. He was writing his life philosophy book *The Choice*, with me, his daughter.[4] But the real reason was that he felt he wasn't done yet uncovering the rules of flow and ensuring that applying them would in fact shorten lead times to an extent that he no longer needed to recommend using buffers for it. He needed a little more time, but he didn't have it. After he passed away in 2011, his work was carried on by the T.O.C. experts at Goldratt Consulting and their affiliates.

My father left me in charge of his books, managing the copyrights, special editions, and so forth with over 30 publishers around the world. After over a decade of highly successful implementations of the rules of flow, and twenty-five years after *Critical Chain* was published, I believe the time has come to tend to the book; the book he wished to write but didn't. When my father wrote *The Goal* I was still in elementary school. But since his second business novel I had the privilege of being part of his inner circle, assisting him in his writing. I am very familiar with his writing style and I know how he would have liked this new book to be written. It is not a rewrite but a brand-new book that pays homage to the original.

Larry Gadd, my father's long-time publisher and editor, offered to edit the book and have it published. Kevin Foster, my colleague and friend, provided valuable insights. But there was an issue. As an Organizational Psychologist I live on the borderline between the individual and organizations, but my focus has always been personal success. Even though I have been teaching the thinking processes of the Theory of Constraints and practicing its application for the individual for years, my background in the application for project management was theoretical. My husband, Dr. Yishai Ashlag, Dr. Ajai Kapoor, and Yossi Reinhartz stepped in to fill in the blanks. It is thanks to their extensive knowledge, ample experience (and buckets of patience...) that every single example in this book is based on real-life cases.

Dr. Efrat Goldratt-Ashlag

1   The Big Picture

Isaac Wilson, the owner of Wilson Advanced Solutions, is sitting at his desk staring at the email on his computer screen. Some legal jargon about poor service and breaching agreed-upon terms, with the last line: "We will no longer be using your services."

This is a heavy blow.

The email is from Doolen, one of their best customers. A large company that has been doing business with them for over fifteen years. They had provided some brilliant solutions for Doolen. He didn't think it would come to this. Doolen should have stayed with them. He had read the email again and again. If they could lose Doolen, the writing was on the wall.

Isaac is proud of the family company he started over three decades ago. But times are changing, things are not as they used to be, and he is not well. He had gotten the diagnosis a while ago and needs to get his affairs in order. He will not leave his family a sinking ship.

Marc exits the gym, his hair still damp from the shower. Glancing at his phone he notices an unanswered call from his father. He should stop at his office and see what this is about. It's early in the morning, but the sun is already blazing and Marc is sweating by the time he gets to his SUV. August just started and it seems like it's going to be a long month.

"Good morning, Dad," Marc calls from the door. Isaac raises his eyes. "Come on in." He gestures to the chair across from his desk. "We need to talk."

Marc Wilson is thirty-two years old, tall, and athletic. Half the age of his father but his spitting image in every other way. To Isaac's delight, Marc joined the company right after getting his degree in engineering. He worked his way up to managing their integration and support teams, and a couple of years ago Isaac put him in charge of his pride and joy, their engineering department.

"Did you manage to mend fences with Doolen?" Marc asks.

"I'm afraid we lost them," Isaac says. "We delivered too late."

"Damn. We missed the final due date only by a month or so."

Isaac tells himself to calm down. "You mean the final, final due date. The one we pushed for after getting two extensions from the original due date." Then he adds, "And it wasn't the first time we missed with them."

"And there was nothing you could do?" Marc persists. "We're working on three other projects for them."

Isaac sees no point in going into details, although he had gotten an earful from Doolen's president, who had become a friend, in their last meeting. "We caused them a serious delay getting their new production line operational. They are done with us."

Isaac braces himself. This conversation is not going to be easy, no matter how he goes about it. "How are we doing with the other projects?"

Marc doesn't want to commit. "We're working as hard as we can."

Isaac is not happy with the answer. "Are we going to meet the deadlines on the B120 and P831?"

These projects are for two other large customers, and both are due next month.

"We'll pick up the pace on them now," Marc replies. "We had all hands on deck to help with Doolen's project."

Isaac sighs. Rushing to finish projects at the very last minute has become the norm and they are missing more and more due dates.

Isaac knows how hard it is to run the engineering department. He ran it from the beginning, until Marc replaced him. Marc had earned his respect for the innovative ideas he came up with and his ability to steer the other engineers in promising directions. Deep inside, Isaac had been hoping that Marc would also figure out some kind of miracle to manage engineering more efficiently, but that doesn't seem to be the case.

"Doolen leaving is a hard hit," Isaac presses on, "and they are not the first ones to go."

"The customers' expectations are unrealistic," Marc replies. "You know these lead times are too short."

"Marc, we're already committing to deliver in six months instead of five. We can't push the due dates any farther."

Marc knows his father is right. Their customers won't tolerate longer lead times. They'll simply go to their competitors. It's not enough time but they will have to make it work.

"Got it," he says, even though he has no idea how they can possibly do better.

"I'm afraid you don't," Isaac replies. "We need to look at the big picture here."

"The big picture?" Marc raises an eyebrow.

Isaac takes his time before answering. He recalls how he opened the business in the old warehouse at the end of town, using his engineering background and software experience to hook cameras and other sensors to industrial robotic arms. Over the years, they kept at the forefront of the rapidly developing technology and software. The small company earned its reputation by conceptualizing, customizing, producing, and integrating cutting edge automation solutions. He kept engineering as well as most other departments in town. The production was moved to the Southeast a few years back when they opened their second location there.

Isaac knows that his son is used to looking at things from the point of view of his department, but he needs to make him see the big picture now.

"The longer lead times and added employees depleted our margins, profits are down, and that negatively affects the company's valuation. Our wide customer base and our reputation also have a lot of bearing on the company's value, and both are at risk. With the increasing competition and the large companies taking over the market, we need to face the fact that we are struggling to keep up."

Marc is baffled. "I'm not sure what else you want me to do."

"I don't think there is much else you can do, son," Isaac says with a heavy heart. "That's why I'm going to start looking for a buyer."

2 | Can't Miss the Due Dates

Marc tries to argue, but his father won't hear any of it. He leaves his father's office and passes by Sophia, the office manager, who just got in. Sophia is a single mom in her late forties who has been running his father's office for many years. Usually he would stop to ask how she and her teenage son are doing. He doesn't mean to be rude, but he is not in the mood to chat now.

He is headed to their conference room. He needs room to pace and his office isn't large enough. Marc is sick to his stomach. What on earth has gotten into his father? He wonders if his sister is in the loop. He should call her. On second thought, he doesn't particularly like talking with his bossy sister. He'll try to deal with their father on his own for now.

If he wants a chance to start the discussion with his father again, he can't miss the due date with these two large customers. He texts Abbie and Kyle, the engineers in charge of these projects, to meet him.

"What's up, Marc?" Kyle is the first one to join him. Kyle

is a bright engineer in his twenties, with excellent management skills. Despite his youth Marc has been giving him more responsibilities and made him the manager on this important project.

"We have to meet the due date on the B120," Marc says, referring to the project Kyle is in charge of.

"Ask for a new due date that will give us a few more weeks, and we'll meet it." Kyle doesn't miss a beat.

"We're not asking for a few more weeks. We need to deliver on time."

"Well, we are not going to make it. You know it's not all our fault. They changed the requirements when we were halfway through. We're going to miss the due date."

"We can't let that happen." Marc sees Abbie at the door and brings the two project managers up to speed.
"We've lost Doolen. We can't afford to piss off any more customers."

"Geez. That's bad news," Abbie says.

The men watch Abbie as she picks a chair and joins them. She is short, a bit on the chubby side, with shoulder length black hair and blue, almond-shaped eyes. Abbie is their mechanical expert and their most capable project manager. She was in charge of Doolen's projects as well as a few others, including the P831 they need to deliver pretty soon.

"I'm sorry, Abbie. I know you did everything you could," says Marc.

Kyle, looking after his own interests, says, "Then give me the people that were working on Doolen's projects."

"No problem," says Abbie, "but don't count on them being of much help. They are already swamped with too many other projects, including the P831."

"Perhaps we dedicate a couple of them to Kyle?" Marc wonders aloud. "It's only for a few weeks."

"That will pretty much guarantee we'll be late on the other stuff they're working on," Abbie says quietly. "We have to get more people."

"We already tried that a year ago," Marc says. "We got more budget and hired good engineers. We increased our staff by ten percent and... and it didn't seem to make any difference."

Marc knows they have to make do with what they've got. They can't hire more people because the numbers won't work.

"Fine," Kyle shrugs. "Let me contact the customer and ask them to cut some features."

Here we go again, Marc is thinking. *Meeting the due dates, staying on budget, and delivering the full scope. It's the same old thing. Everyone knows that when we start a new project, we aim to get all three of these requirements, but as the project progresses, we end up having to choose. If we want to meet one of these requirements, we end up compromising on one or two of the others. The reality of projects. Always has been.* Only now he cannot afford to compromise on any of them.

"Listen, we can't risk losing any more customers. We have to do better. Whatever it takes."

"I don't know how much more we can take." Kyle is weary. "People already put in a lot of hours. We practically live here."

Abbie says, "We're done here, right?"

"Yeah."

"I better tell the people to stop working on Doolen's projects," she says as she stands up.

Kyle is taking his time. He is burned out and it's not worth it. The company seems to be struggling and he doesn't want any stains on his immaculate résumé. But he wishes to stay on good terms with the Wilsons. They have been good to him, and he may need references.

"Marc, can I have a word with you?" Kyle says after Abbie leaves the room. "I've been meaning to talk with you, and it might as well be now."

"Talk with me about what?"

"The thing is I've got another offer. One that is too good to pass up. So please understand, but I would like to give you my four weeks' notice."

3 | Re-evaluating

Marc works late most evenings, but it's Friday night and he needs a break. He drives downtown and enters a nice, upscale bar. As he makes his way to an empty stool he notices there are quite a few good-looking women there. It has been awhile since he was involved with someone. A slower look around the room reveals the women are all in tight groups, laughing and having fun. He doesn't want to intrude. Meeting a girl at a bar is not as easy as it sounds, and he can't stand the swiping game on dating apps.

The bartender approaches Marc and catches him looking at the whiskey shelf. "Why don't you treat yourself to something nice?" he says, and reaches for a fourteen-year-old single malt.

"I might as well," Marc answers and goes back to his thoughts.

This wasn't the plan at all. He never thought he'd end up alone. After graduating he had joined the family company and totally immersed himself in work. The long hours and frequent traveling to customers made time fly, but he was lonely. He kept putting off his plans to see the world. It was just never the right timing to take time off from work. He didn't even get the business degree he desired. And now it looked like all this effort was not going to pay off. He wouldn't become the head of the family company, simply because there wouldn't be a family company.

Marc takes another sip of his whiskey and feels the smooth fire going down his throat. He is not going to give up. He'll find a way to change his father's mind. But then what? As much as he hates to admit it, his father may have a point.

You're not a quitter, Marc says to himself, and looks up. The bartender puts nice-looking appetizers in front of the couple sitting on his left. He will stay with the company and do his best, but he needs to start thinking of himself as well.

Why don't you treat yourself to something nice? he is thinking. *Why not?* The dream of hiking across Australia will have to be put off for obvious reasons. But maybe it's time to get his MBA? He has been thinking about that for a while now. He can go to the local university, so he won't need to leave town. They have weekend classes every other week, so it won't interfere much with work. That means he'll sign up for the Executive MBA program. He likes the sound of that. The company will pay for it. His father owes him at least that.

"I'll take another one," he says to the bartender. "I'm treating myself to something nice."

4   Undesirable Effects in Multi-Project Environments

September arrives and the academic year begins. Rick enters the classroom and puts his leather bag on the professor's desk. The Rules of Flow course in the Executive MBA program is his favorite. Since he started teaching this course over ten years ago, he has gotten a lot of experience in the field and the material has developed quite a bit, but the first lecture has remained the same.

He looks around. About twenty students are in the room and as usual the first row is empty. Everybody is quiet, except for a small group in the back that is too busy talking to notice he is about to start.

"My name is Professor Richard Silver, and you are?" Rick attempts to grab the attention of the woman who is talking in the back. She has big glasses and thick black hair tied in a ponytail.

"Kiara Srini." She turns to Rick and sits down. "Sorry about that," she apologizes.

"Do you happen to work in a multi-project environment?" Rick asks her. The students better realize from the get-go that his teaching style is different.

"You could say that." She smiles and gestures to the other two in her group. "We work for the IT division of a bank." She goes on as if she's used to explaining. "Our division develops and maintains all the bank's information technology needs. Everything the bank employees and customers do online."

"Perfect," Rick says. IT departments have a lot of room for improvement. Good that she brought reinforcements. He turns to the rest of the class. "Who else operates in a multi-project environment?"

The room is quiet. Rick looks around. No one volunteers.

Finally, an elegant woman with perfect makeup and not a hair out of place, the only person sitting in the second row, asks, "Can you explain what you mean by 'multi-project'?"

"Sure." Rick is glad she asked. "And you are?"

"Shonda James."

Knowing that the academic definitions won't be very helpful here, Rick opts to reply with a question. "Are you involved in more than one project that share common resources?"

"I believe so," she answers. "I'm in marketing. My department is responsible for launching all the campaigns for my company's new products."

"Excellent."

"I'm Ted, and I'm the general manager at a construction company," says a freckled redhead in the corner. "We work on several projects in parallel and we juggle some resources between them."

Someone makes a sarcastic remark about contractors and juggling that Rick chooses to ignore. "Definitely multi-project. Who else?"

Soon it becomes apparent that pretty much everyone in the class is involved in one way or another with multiple projects. Kiara and her colleagues from IT, Ted in construction, Shonda in marketing, Marc who runs the engineering department in his family company, and a group of rather young guys in plaid flannel shirts who work at a nearby software company. Rick is familiar with the amazing salaries and perks young programmers get these days. These guys probably got the MBA program as a bonus or something.

Good, Rick says to himself. *That variety is going to make it interesting. We can start.*

Rick grabs a marker from his bag and writes as high as he can on the whiteboard. "Undesirable Effects in Project Management." He could have written "things that annoy you on a regular basis," but he needs to sound academic.

He turns back to the class. "Kiara, will you please share with us what the heated discussion earlier was about?" The group was rather loud, and Rick had overheard enough to figure it was work-related.

Kiara's colleague who sits on her left answers. "We've got this issue we've been struggling with for a while now, and Kiara's people could probably figure it out in a week. But she said they don't have time to help us."

Kiara explains in an apologetic tone, "My unit designed the infrastructure for the current version, so it is easier for us to figure these things out. I am trying to help everyone as much as I can, but my people are pulled in so many directions that we hardly have enough time to work on our own assignments."

The man on her right comes to her defense. "One of Kiara's people was helping us last month and he was constantly interrupted by other urgent matters. He kept going back and forth between us and other teams, so what we thought would take him a few days to fix ended up taking three weeks."

"Leaving your people hanging while they waited to get the issue resolved?" Rick wants to make a point.

"Are you kidding? With the current workload? We're all going back and forth between tasks. They worked on other stuff, but this issue was urgent."

Rick says aloud as he is writing on the whiteboard, "People are forced into bad multitasking." Everyone nods in agreement. "Thanks for sharing," he says to the group in the back. "Who else has issues that interfere with running their projects smoothly?"

Charlie, one of the youngsters in the plaid shirts, calls, "Rework! We get a piece of software nearly done, and then they change the specs, and we have to start all over again."

Charlie's friends offer several examples. All Rick gets is they have a few "enemies" who keep changing the specifications.

Rick writes "there is too much rework" on the whiteboard.

Ted, the construction guy, calls from the corner. "We actually don't mind when the customers ask for changes. That means we get to charge them more."

No one appreciates his remark, so he continues. "What

we can't stand is the need for approvals. We get going, the people, machinery, and materials are on site, and then we have to wait for inspections and permits. Work just comes to a halt."

Rick smiles; this one always comes up in the top three complaints. He writes in general terms, "too often work comes to a halt because relatively small things (approvals/ people/materials...) are missing."

"I have another one." Shonda raises her hand. 'Too much time is spent on status reports."

"I know exactly what you're talking about," Kiara says. "We have to be in so many meetings to follow up on where people stand and how we are doing with the budget, et cetera, that sometimes it feels like we don't have enough time to work."

Rick writes "too much time is spent on status reports" on the whiteboard.

The discussion moves on to other complaints and Rick writes, "there are fights about priorities between projects," "there are budget overruns," and "original due dates are not met." A couple more undesirable effects and he runs out of space on the whiteboard. Time to move on.

"I'm glad everyone is pitching in," Rick says. "Did you notice that no matter what field you come from, the problems in project management are basically the same?"

"And not much can be done about it," someone adds.

"Life's a bitch and then we die," Charlie, the young software guy, says with a heavy sigh. Everybody smiles.

"Here's the thing." Rick seizes the opportunity. "The common wisdom in project management sure gives that impression. The literature is full of optimization techniques, complicated heuristics, and comprehensive surveys. This material is hard to understand and even harder to implement. It will probably leave you with the notion that not much can be done about the way you manage projects, beyond what you're already doing." Rick gestures to Charlie and continues. "In this course we'll cover Goldratt's approach to multi-project environments, which is part of his Theory of Constraints. Implementing this approach takes a lot of discipline, but it also gets results."

"You won't be reviewing the conventional literature?" Marc asks.

"No. That is covered in the project management course," Rick replies. "If you think you're in the wrong course, now would be the time to switch."

Sounds like a sales pitch of an arrogant professor. Marc keeps this thought to himself. Maybe he *should* switch courses. At least he would get a good understanding of what's out there in the field, and not a specific application of a unique theory. But the project management course is at eight o'clock in the morning and he doesn't want to miss his Saturday workout at the gym.

Rick looks at his watch. The discussion about undesirable effects took too long. He needs to switch gears. "Our objective is to improve performance. Get more projects completed on time, within the original budget, while meeting the full scope." He establishes the common ground. "To achieve that, we should ascertain the obstacles that obstruct the flow of projects." Rick points to the whiteboard behind him.

"The obstacles that are causing all those undesirable effects."

Rick looks around; it seems that everyone is still with him. The concept of flow is pretty straightforward. It's easy to visualize the stream of projects going through the system and understand that if something clogs the flow, the projects pile up. The lead time gets longer and as a result the reliability of due dates suffers. It is also easy to understand that obstacles limit the number of projects that can go through, and often hurts their quality.

He continues, "In this course we will cover several obstacles to projects' flow and reveal the 'Rules of Flow' to better manage multi-project environments. As we proceed, you will see which of the rules of flow is more relevant to improving the performance of your multi-project environment."

Rick takes a breath and keeps going. "The first obstacle to flow I'd like to cover is wasting resources."

"Sorry?" Shonda says out loud what everyone is probably thinking.

"Let me ask you, Shonda," Rick turns to her, "what would you say about a team who is under a lot of pressure to complete their projects, and yet they devote a portion of their time to a project that requires them to..." Rick is looking for a good example "...type gibberish?"

Shonda retorts, "I would say they are wasting their resources. Are you suggesting that this is what we do?"

"I'm suggesting you make sure you don't."

Shonda's voice gets a bit high. "Well, I can assure you everything we do is useful."

"I'm not so sure about that," says Charlie. "Some of the

features we're asked to work on seem pretty useless to me."

"Thank you, Charlie." Rick turns to face the rest of the students. "Think about it. A lot of us work on projects that cannot be measured directly in terms of income. It makes sense to verify that the dollars and hours we spend bring value to the company."

The class is quiet. People in project environments are not used to thinking in terms of value.

Rick wants to steer them in the right direction. "Think about the objective of your company and its strategy to achieve it. Are the projects you are working on helpful in getting your company to achieve its goals? Do your projects bring value to your company's customers?"

Rick knows there are differences between for-profit and nonprofit organizations and between companies who sell their projects directly to their customers and departments who supply their projects inside the company, but he is out of time. "I'd like you to entertain the idea of value while working on your homework," he says.

No matter what the age of the students, the reaction is always the same: a deep sigh.

Rick has no mercy. "For your first homework assignment you get to triage."

5 What is Triage

It's nine o'clock on Thursday night. Marc is still in his office. The rain is pounding on the small window that takes up most of the wall behind him. The door is open so he feels less claustrophobic and he can see some of his people are still there, trying to make headway with the late projects. They are probably the only ones left in the building. It's been a long week and Marc is tired, but he can't call it a day yet. The homework for the Rules of Flow course is due today, which means he has three more hours before he has to post it.

I better do something about it, he says to himself, and turns to his computer. He isn't particularly impressed with Professor Silver, but homework is homework, and he wants to get the credits for this course.

Marc opens the project reports file. He keeps a close eye on these projects. They are currently working on thirty-four of them. This number is up to date, after Doolen's three projects were deleted, and the new ones they got since have been entered. They managed to complete the P831 and B120 on time. Barely. But they are late on four other projects.

Professor Silver asked them to triage. This term is borrowed from the medical field. It means that in situations with a large number of patients or casualties, the limited medical staff is compelled to prioritize; to sort the wounded or ill and treat them according to the severity of their condition. The ones who need urgent care are treated first. Some patients can wait, and some don't need to be treated at all. If, for example, the medics find three people in an ambulance, covered in blood, it might be a waste of resources to get all three of them beds. Two of them may be the injured person's friends who tried to help and got his blood all over them. Actually, maybe none of them needs treatment, if the injured person has already passed away.

Triage is not only about prioritizing but also about deciding what is the right course of treatment. If someone is having a heart attack, they clearly need to be treated by a cardiologist, not by an orthopedist. And when someone who doesn't need an MRI is sent to get one, it's clearly a waste of resources. It may also delay the proper treatment and possibly harm the patient. Triage is done in the best interest of the patients and in attempt not to waste resources but rather utilize them in the most efficient manner.

"In projects," Professor Silver had explained, "it makes sense to triage because we also work with limited resources relative to the demand."

That, for sure, is true in our case, Marc is thinking. His people are under constant pressure to get everything done, and there is never enough time or enough people.

Marc looks at his report. The projects are listed in order of due date, with the ones that are the most overdue at the top. It's clear that too many projects are late or dangerously close to being late, and these are the ones with top priority. But he doesn't think they are wasting resources. Marc makes sure that the experienced project managers work on the more complicated projects and when there is a need he gets them more people to help out.

Now what? Marc is trying to think in terms of bringing value. He is not sure how to go about it. Professor Silver didn't go into details. Marc shrugs. All their projects have value: they help their customers' production become safer, more precise, and much more efficient, and they bring revenue to Wilson. All the proposals they write and time they spend on proof of concepts also have value; it's their way to get new projects.

I need to write something, Marc tells himself as he wearily skims the projects. One of them catches his eye. This is a request for a proposal they received from a company that rarely does business with them. This customer has asked them to work on similar proposals in the past and always ended up signing with one of their competitors. Marc has a distinct feeling they only use Wilson as a reference. This one probably has low value for them.

Marc takes a little break to stretch his back and then looks back at the screen. The project at the very bottom doesn't have an assigned due date. This is a small project that one of his electronic engineers came up with. The man thought his idea would be an awesome solution to pitch to a customer, once it's completed. He had a lot of ownership in his idea, and Marc approved it to motivate him. *This one is a long shot*, Marc thinks.

That will do. He writes a short report and hits the send button. Homework is done.

As he is getting ready to leave, Marc thinks about these two projects. Both of them are rather small, they have little to no value, but they will take up some man hours to complete. It won't alleviate the pressure his people are under by much, but nevertheless it makes sense to put them on the back burner.

Marc exits the building and walks to his SUV. It's very dark outside but at least it has stopped raining. He knows the engineers who are working on these two projects won't appreciate hearing that they have to put aside something they are invested in. His people are upset with him anyway. All he has done lately is push them to work harder and faster.

Abbie would know how to approach them, he is thinking. But he is the one who needs to take care of this.

6 | Triage in Practice

"I'm glad to see everyone is here," says Rick. It's a beautiful Saturday morning, might be the last one this fall, and the temptation to be outside is almost physical.

The students settle down, so Rick gets going. "I have reviewed the homework," he begins, and looks at Kiara. "The IT group assignment was very impressive. Kiara, why don't you tell us more about it?"

"Well," Kiara arranges her thoughts as she is making her way to the front of the class, "let me give you some background first. Most small to midsize banks buy their software from outside providers, but larger banks and us included, develop their own. Our IT division's budget is roughly two hundred million dollars a year, and we have about one thousand people. We deal with projects, or 'work packages' as we call them, that greatly vary in size, from the next gen, the infrastructure of our next generation software, all the way to fixing small bugs. We have modifications and new features and the ongoing updates of our phone applications. We take care of change requests, like 'please enable access to this function from over there,' and the never-ending changes in regulations. Regulations are not a small thing–incorporating new regulations into the software accounts for about twenty-five percent of our workload."

Kiara takes a breath and continues, "Just to give you a rough idea, if we sum up all the man-month estimates to accomplish what we need to do in a given time, the demand comes to about five hundred percent more than our people can handle. So we definitely match your description, Professor Silver, of having 'limited resources relative to the demand.'"

Rick looks around. He has had a fair share of students from insurance, banking, and credit card companies in the past, so he is used to these numbers in IT divisions, but the class sure is impressed. Everyone is quiet, waiting for Kiara to go on.

"As far as thinking in terms of value, we weren't sure how to start. The way we work now is, everyone who wants something from IT submits a request by June, our budget is approved by December, so we know what to work on next year."

Kiara's righthand man tries to help her from the back of the room. "We never thought about it as typing gibberish, but between us, we have been thinking that some of the work packages we are working on contribute little to nothing."

Kiara's other colleague jumps in. "You wouldn't believe some of the stuff we are asked to do. People who have problems handling customers, or managing their teams or whatever, immediately think the way to fix it is by adding another feature. Often those features don't make any difference."

"So, it makes sense to triage the projects according to their value," Rick concludes. "How did you end up going about it?"

"Well," Kiara says, "we know that the goal of our bank is to make money through bringing value to our customers. So, we thought the IT department should support that."

"Excellent," Rick encourages her.

"For example," Kiara continues, "we invest a lot of effort in digitizing documents. Whenever customers open an account, apply for a loan, or basically do anything, they need to fill out quite a lot of paperwork. That is a known hassle for the customers and digitizing it just means they will fill all the blanks and sign in all the marked places online instead of on paper. When we started thinking in terms of value to the customer, it became apparent that we should change the scope of this mammoth project and do our best to reduce the redundancies and minimize the number of documents."

"Duh!" Ted mutters, just loud enough for Kiara to hear. "Why on earth would you require us to fill in our details four or five times?!"

Kiara gestures to him, trying to be nice. "We believe we can get it down significantly."

Kiara's righthand man adds, "Many work packages in IT are inward-looking, aiming to address internal organizational needs and optimize working procedures. Typically, it is hard to evaluate their effectiveness or contribution. So, as a rule of thumb, we decided to give priority to projects that can clearly demonstrate tangible benefits to the bank's customers."

"Here's another thing," Kiara adds. "When we started

thinking in terms of value, we realized we should also look into the specs inside the work packages."

Marc's ears perk up. He hadn't thought about the specifications.

Kiara says, "Many specs are added just because someone thought they would be nice to have or because of a rare instance where they might be needed someday."

"Or because someone wanted to feel they were contributing," says Kiara's colleague.

Kiara smiles at her, acknowledging her contribution. "So, we assigned some people to look into it in some urgent projects, and found loads of specs with low value." Kiara pauses for a minute. "Just think about your bank's website." She looks around the class. "What percentage of its features do you actually use?"

Everyone smiles. Kiara is laughing. "And I bet many of you are not aware of the new features that are being added all the time."

She says, "Reviewing all of our work packages through the lens of bringing value to our customers, and looking for clear benefits in our internal improvement efforts, reveals we are wasting a lot of resources on work packages that have little to no value. Triage will free a lot of resources and help us focus our work on the more important things."

Kiara's colleague adds, "Needless to say that we need to continue to triage the new assignments on an ongoing basis. So, moving forward we plan to put together clear guidelines for people to know how to justify future work packages they would like IT to work on."

Kiara concludes, "Having so many work packages, the triage is a lot of work, but we are making headway."

Rick is surprised. Given the politics involved, he was expecting to hear about bloody battles at this point.

"People's personal agendas don't get in the way?" he asks.

"Oh, for sure," Kiara says. "I need to explain something. We are not alone. The vice president in charge of our division is looking into implementing Goldratt's approach. We were chosen to do the groundwork, and our manager and the VP above him will handle the politics when it's over our heads."

"That makes sense," Rick smiles. "Political considerations may completely distort the priorities and it takes someone high enough and tough enough to handle them."

"Our VP sure fits that description," declares Kiara's colleague.

"Well done," Rick compliments the IT group as Kiara returns to her seat. Then he turns to the class. "In this type of a multi-project environment, wasting resources is the first obstacle to flow we should consider. And the rule of flow to apply here is triage. Triage requires work but it provides a lot of clarity as far as what needs to be done in what priority and by which resources."

Rick pauses for a minute and then continues, "When you triage, make sure that the projects with low value, especially the ones which require a lot of effort, are canceled."

"Knowing the dynamics in our company," says Charlie, "they would like to avoid confrontations with the people who suggested the low-value features, so they probably won't cancel them. They will simply assign them a lower priority."

"And?" Rick asks, predicting what happens next.

29

Charlie shrugs. "And we will be expected to work on them from time to time, so basically nothing will change."

"That is precisely why we shouldn't do that," Rick says. "The low-value projects should not be placed lower on the list but rather should be completely canceled."

"Also," Rick continues, "as you saw in the IT case, it is crucial that the triage be done by the right people; people with a deep understanding of the situation and the projects, and also with the power to handle the political issues."

"You bet," Kiara says. "I have to say it's a challenge. This is all very different from how we're operating now. We are used to thinking mainly in terms of budget."

Rick agrees. "And this will probably lead you to consider another big challenge. Switching from a predetermined yearly budget to allocating the budget per project throughout the year." Rick has a lot more to say about that, but he reminds himself that this lecture is about triage.

"Thank you, Kiara."

Rick would have liked to review everyone's homework in class. The more examples the students see, the better they understand the different aspects of triage. But he has time for only one more.

Rick turns to Ted, the construction guy, who had seemed rather uninterested until now. "I'd like to commend you on a new record, Ted. The shortest homework ever."

Rick tells the class that Ted has submitted two digits and two letters.

Ted says, "That pretty much covers it. We currently have fourteen construction projects, and 'NR' means just that. The whole triage thing is not relevant to us."

To Ted's surprise, Rick agrees. "For companies like yours, who sell their projects directly to the end consumer, every project means incoming revenue. I assume that your company knows how to choose the right projects that give you the most profit, so, you're right, there is value in all the projects and there is no need to triage."

Rick turns to the class and explains. "However, in multi-project environments where the projects are not sold directly to the customers, one of the first obstacles to flow we need to look into is wasting resources. With the pressure that we are under, let's make sure we're not typing gibberish, but rather that we prioritize and spend our resources on valuable projects. That is why I cover the triage first."

Marc keeps quiet. He hadn't found many low-value projects, and he certainly did not uncover loads of waste like Kiara had. In essence, their engineering department is probably more similar to Ted's company than to Kiara's, but the concept makes sense.

Rick can tell the class is with him, so he moves on. "The next topic we are going to cover is bound to be relevant to everyone. For your homework, I'd like you to submit a report on the consequences of multitasking."

7 | Removing the "Nice-to-Haves"

"Sir, would you like some orange juice or water?" the flight attendant is asking with a red lipstick smile as she is moving down the aisle with a tray full of glasses.

It's Friday afternoon. Marc is relaxing in his business class seat. He is flying over to spend the weekend with his sister and her family. Marc needs to talk with Samantha about their father's alarming plan. Sam has been running their company's production for years. She and her family had moved to the Southeast when Wilson opened their second location there. She runs their new production facility in addition to a small sales team and a local integration and support department. Marc doesn't mind having more physical distance between him and his sister, but he misses her kids terribly. He loves his nephew and niece and it has been months since he saw them last, at Sam's fortieth birthday party.

"What would you like to eat, sir?" The flight attendant is back. "We have two choices today."

Marc had used his frequent flyer points for an upgrade so he wouldn't be squeezed in a coach seat, but he doesn't care for all the flight attendant's fussing around.

"No, thanks. I'll pass." Marc assures her he is fine. He plugs in his headphones and turns on the noise cancellation. They are about to take off.

It's been a busy week and he's beat. In addition to his usual load Marc had a long one-on-one with each of his seven project managers. He had stopped having those meetings when things got hectic, and he could tell that was a mistake. After catching up with them and hearing the latest updates on their work, he emphasized the importance of meeting the deadlines. In an attempt to save time, Marc suggested they review the specs in their projects and determine if all of them were inherently necessary. They spotted a few specs that the engineers added themselves. They approved a couple of them that seemed important, but the rest were basically "nice-to-haves" and were removed.

One of the project managers indicated that they were working on a project where the requirements requested by the customer seemed excessive. They got on a conference call with the customer, who sounded surprised by this inquiry so early in the process. He asked for some time to consult with his people and emailed back a couple of days later confirming the removal of most of the "nice-to-haves" from the list of requirements, but warned them not to ask for any more cuts once they got closer to the deadline.

Marc had met with Abbie that morning to evaluate the specs in her projects and review the week's effort. Between canceling the two projects that Marc spotted in his triage and trimming the specs, they had gained a little time. Too little to matter.

I have to do more, Marc is thinking. *We're running late on more and more projects.*

Abbie, bless her, had put together a memo with their new guidelines: The project managers must approve specs that are not directly related to the customer's requirements. And Marc has to be part of every phone call to a customer, if they suspect too many "nice-to-haves" were requested. Marc needs to make sure they're not upsetting anyone; he doesn't want any surprises here. He had emailed Abbie's memo to everyone before he left the office.

Marc closes his eyes. Enough about work. As he is falling asleep his thoughts wander to Abbie. He knows she is about his age. He wonders if she is single.

Marc steps through the automatic door into the arrivals area and easily spots Dave, his nephew. Dave is as tall as his mother but thin as a rail. A big hug and they head to the parking lot.

"I can't believe you're old enough to drive." Marc attempts to mess Dave's hair.

Dave dodges his reach and tells him everything about the Jeep he got from his parents for his sixteenth birthday.

"Where's your sister?" Marc asks as they fasten their seatbelts.

Dave says she is out on a date.

"You have got to be kidding me!" Marc is choking. "She's eleven!"

"Do you seriously think I'd let her go on a date?" Dave is laughing. He gets Marc every time. "She's home making you a surprise cake."

"No worries," Marc assures him. "I'll act surprised."

The Jeep is comfortable, and Dave is a good driver. They leave the airport and make their way to his sister's fancy house in one of the luxury gated communities at the edge of town. Dave turns on the audio system. They have similar taste and Dave updates Marc on the latest music.

The following morning Marc and Sam, both dressed in white, are playing tennis at the nearby private club. Marc does his best, but as expected, Sam wins. After the match they walk over to the patio outside the clubhouse to refresh themselves with some ice tea.

Once they sit down, Marc says, "Do you know about Dad's plan to sell the company?"

"Yes." Sam is not shaken by the news. "If the old man wants to sell the company, he should sell the company."

"But it's the family company!" Marc exclaims.

"The fact that you and I are working for Dad does not make it the family company," Sam says. "It's his company and he can do whatever he wants with it."

Marc tries to hide his disappointment. He had been hoping for some support. "So, what are your plans?"

"We're staying here," Sam answers. "Jack will make partner soon, and the kids love it here. If I don't like working for whoever buys the company, I'll go work for someone else. There are a lot of production facilities around. I'd get a new job in no time."

Marc had always known his sister had no aspirations of managing Wilson Advance Solutions once their father retired. He made sure that was the case years ago, but only now he realizes how little sense of ownership she has in the company. For her, it's just a job. One she can easily get elsewhere. Well, this is not the case for him. He sees himself as an integral part of the family company, and he really wants to take over and keep it going once their father retires.

Marc is contemplating whether to argue or let it go when Sam gets a phone call. It sounds to Marc like there is some sort of crisis at the factory. He is crossing his fingers it has nothing to do with his department. His sister complains about them all the time.

"We have to go." Sam offers to drop Marc at the house as she has to change. She had been planning to stay at home today and host her brother, but work comes first.

In a way, Marc is glad that Sam had to leave. Being eight years older she has never really treated him as an equal. He has no idea how she ended up with a great husband and two wonderful kids. The opportunity to spend the afternoon alone with his niece and nephew is a treat. They have a great time playing in the swimming pool and goofing around. When Sam comes back in time for dinner Marc is relieved to hear the issue in the factory had nothing to do with him.

It's amazing how time flies when you're relaxing. On Sunday afternoon Marc is on the flight home. As far as changing their father's mind, it is now clear that he is on his own.

8 Bad Multitasking

The following Saturday morning, Rick is walking to class, wondering if he should use an animated presentation for this lecture. He has a whole collection of these, given to him by former students who had used the material in their organizations. Nah, he likes to keep it simple, he'll use the whiteboard. That's the prerogative of being a professor; no one tells him what to do.

Rick enters the classroom. Everyone is in their seats waiting for him to start. He writes "the effect of bad multi-tasking" on the whiteboard and turns to the students. "Reviewing your homework," he opens up, "there is a consensus that multitasking is a necessary evil. Under the current workload and the pressure to make progress, it is necessary for most, if not all of us, to go back and forth between projects."

Rick looks around, making sure everyone is with him. "There is also a consensus that multitasking causes a lot of aggravation. It promotes conflicts and fights over resources shared by different projects. It contributes to people's fatigue and burnout, and fosters mistakes. That is all correct, but it's only the tip of the iceberg. I'd like to talk about what lies below the surface. The problem with multitasking is that it's the biggest killer of time that exists in projects."

What a dramatic statement, Marc thinks. But the professor has his attention.

Rick turns to the whiteboard and starts drawing. "Let's look at a simple example where we have three projects, each of which takes nine days to complete."

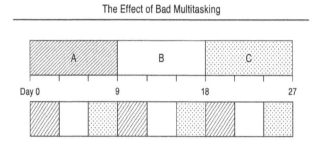

The Effect of Bad Multitasking

Rick points to the top row. "Here there is no multitasking. So, we start working on project A on day one, and complete it in nine days. We start working on project B on the tenth day and complete it in nine days, and we only start working on project C on the nineteenth day, but we also complete it in nine days."

Rick proceeds, "In the bottom row, the squares indicate we multitask between the projects. We start with project A, but after completing only a third of it, we switch to work on project B, and after completing only a third of B, we switch to project C, et cetera. As above, we start working on project A on day one, but look what happens to its lead time."

"No way!" Shonda is stunned. "Project A will take twenty-one days, instead of nine!"

Ted states the obvious. "Projects look so simple only in this imaginary diagram. In reality, unexpected delays always happen." No one pays attention to him.

Marc is speechless. That is precisely what's going on in his department. He tries to visualize the line of squares on the whiteboard when multitasking between thirty-something projects. No wonder that even their simplest project takes forever to complete.

Rick wants to make sure everyone got the point. "The major factor that impacts the lead time is the number of projects we multitask between. The more projects in the mix the longer the lead time."

Rick waits for a minute to let the message sink in and then he adds, "In this example we haven't included any set-up time, but this is rarely the case in reality. Think about yourself when you multitask. When you return to a project you didn't work on for a while, can you immediately pick up where you left off?"

Shonda says, "Each time I switch to work on another project I have to sift through several files and documents to collect my thoughts. The setup time is certainly not negligible."

"Not negligible?" Ted calls from his corner. "When one of my teams comes back to a project they had to leave, often people don't remember what they are supposed to do next and they have to study the construction plans and get a hold of the architect and then someone remembers the customer asked for a last-minute change but they're not sure if it was added to the plans and no one remembers what it was, so we have to contact the customer. This setup time is definitely not negligible!"

"Not negligible is the understatement of the year!" Charlie calls from the other side of the class. "When I dive into a feature that was put aside, my immediate reaction is, 'which idiot wrote this code?!' Even if that idiot was me, I have no recollection of why I chose to write it the way I did and now I think of a better way to go about it. So I just scratch everything and start over. And of course it doesn't work, and I have to find all the bugs and fix them, and the whole thing takes forever."

"You bet, Charlie." Rick is glad that Charlie brought this up. "It often happens that when we come back to a project we haven't worked on for a while, instead of digging into what was done before, we opt to start over."

Rick points to the whiteboard. "What you are all saying is that in the row of bad multitasking, the lead time is even longer because there should be spaces between the squares that signify setup times and, on occasion, rework."
Rick pauses for the dramatic effect of what he's about to say next. "In reality, most of us multitask between more than three projects. So, the lead time of each project is longer than what it should be, not by ten or twenty percent, but by hundreds of percents. This is why I refer to multitasking as the biggest killer of time."

The class is quiet. People are seldom aware of the devastating effect that multitasking has on time.

Marc's mind is racing. *Where is he going with this*? He keeps hearing the professor's words, "the more projects in the mix the longer the lead time."

After a while, Shonda speaks up. "What are you trying to say? We have to go back and forth between projects."

Rick answers her slowly. "I understand. But do we have to go back and forth between so many projects?" Rick turns to the class. "In order to significantly reduce the lead time, what we need to do is control WIP; control the amount of Work In Process, the active projects we are working on at any given time."

Marc wants more than just an acronym. "What do you mean by controlling WIP?" He pronounces "whip" the same way as the professor said it, as a word.

Rick is a bit sorry he didn't upload one of the animated presentations. "What I mean is, you limit the number of projects that you're dealing with in parallel. You bring a new one in only after you have completed one of the projects that you already started."

Makes sense, Marc is thinking. The problem is, his operation is already jammed with too many projects. Right now, things hardly move. If he waits until enough projects are completed before he lets new ones in, he risks releasing the new ones too late.

"What do you do if you have too many projects in the flow to begin with?" Marc asks.

"That's a tough one. If you can't take your time and wait until enough projects are completed, you need to start by freezing some of the projects that you already started to work on; projects that are currently in WIP."

Marc is not sure what that means. "Are you suggesting we let go of some of our projects?"

"I'm suggesting you temporarily freeze them," Rick replies.

Ted is not impressed. "What you're saying is, we decide up front which projects we work on and deliver on time, and which projects we freeze and deliver later than promised."

Rick reminds himself that he doesn't have to love all his students. He doesn't even have to like them. But he does have to care about them and their success.

"Ted, think about it. If you significantly reduce the number of projects you go back and forth between, you will significantly reduce their lead time. That will enable you to finish these projects much faster, and then work on the ones you froze, and finish them much faster as well."

Uncertain faces all around. Rick is calm. He gets this reaction every time.

Shonda, as usual, is looking for details. "How many projects do we have to freeze to considerably shorten the lead time?" she asks.

"You need to freeze enough to get the flow of projects going. In many cases, we have a pretty good sense of the capacity of our system. We know how many projects we can efficiently work on, so it is rather easy to deduce how many we need to freeze."

"And if we don't know?" Shonda persists.

"That usually means the chaos is enormous. You'll probably need to freeze a large percentage of your projects."

"How large?" Marc inquires.

"Some companies start by freezing twenty to thirty percent of their projects. It takes awhile before they notice a reduction in the lead time and the reduction is somewhat limited, but then they feel more comfortable freezing more. In other companies the flow is so clogged that if they freeze only twenty percent of the projects, they will hardly notice any difference. I have seen cases in which companies got the flow of projects going once they froze seventy or eighty percent."

Obviously, this is a drastic change from the current convention in managing projects. The students are quiet, trying to digest.

Rick says, "What's important is to control WIP on an ongoing basis. To see to it that the flow of projects going through your system is fast and efficient. The freeze is a tough pill to swallow, but it is a onetime effort to get the flow going."

Rick can tell that people are still thinking, but there is another important point he needs to make. "The bad multitasking is not only between projects but also between smaller day-to-day tasks. And this form of bad multitasking also consumes our time."

"Oh yeah, you should see me some mornings," Charlie chuckles, happy to ease the tension. "I get to my cubicle and start reviewing my emails. Before I get through half of them, my cellphone is ringing. I put whoever it is on hold, because someone from the next cubicle is calling me. I go over to see if I can help, but I can't really concentrate because I keep thinking about the person who called, but I can't look into what they want because I left my phone next to my seat. I go back to get it and notice an incoming email, which reminds me I didn't finish reading my emails. Before you know it half the morning is over, and I got nothing done."

People are laughing. Everyone knows exactly what

Charlie is talking about. Rick says, "If people keep bouncing from one task to another, running around like chickens who got their heads chopped off, very little gets done. Part of controlling the WIP is also figuring out how to significantly reduce the day-to-day, hour-by-hour multitasking."

"And how do you do that?"

"Simple. You start a task, you complete it before you move on."

Reducing the multitasking on the projects and on the day-to-day level is relevant to everyone. Lots of questions are coming from all directions and Rick answers them patiently, one by one. At some point someone notices their time is up.

Rick summarizes quickly, "One of the biggest obstacles to projects' flow is bad multitasking. It has a negative effect on many factors and a devastating effect on the lead time. To improve the flow, we need to control the work in process we deal with at any given time."

Rick has to release the students, or they will be late for their next class. Never mind, he'll give them plenty of homework next time.

9 | Will it Work?

Will it work? is all Marc can think of. It has been a little over two months since his father dropped the bomb about selling the company. Marc hasn't heard anything concrete, but he knows his father is quietly talking with people in his network. Marc has been racking his brain trying to think of ways to ensure they deliver on time. The weeks have passed, and all he has to show for it is more late projects. After the class on Saturday morning Marc kept thinking about the idea of controlling WIP. He can't find any flaws in the logic. The question is, will it work?

In normal times that would be a perfect question to ask his father. The old man has remarkable intuition and years of experience in projects. But this is not the right time to run such a revolutionary idea by him. He might block the initiative and Marc will lose the chance to try it. Better to ask for forgiveness than for permission, Marc decides.

The next person on his mind is Abbie. He appreciates her opinion and anyway, he'll need her help. Marc had tex-

47

ted Abbie first thing on Monday morning. She should have been there by now. Marc looks again at his cellphone.

Today
"R U available?"
    "Busy. After lunch?"
"Good. My office."

Well, it's two minutes past one. As much as Marc is eager to share his thoughts, it makes sense that Abbie is busy. They are all busy on Monday mornings, fighting fires and reorganizing priorities to get things done.

Abbie shows up a few minutes later.

"Hi Abbie, will you please close the door?" Marc doesn't care about feeling cooped up today. He wants no rumors spreading when they discuss freezing projects.

"Sure." Abbie is a bit surprised. Everybody knows Marc's door is always open. She closes the door and sits on the only other chair, across the desk from Marc.

"Do you mind if I eat while we talk?" she asks as she peels the cover off a plastic box full of salad.

"Not at all," Marc assures her, and goes right ahead. "Abbie, do you think there is more we can do to ensure we deliver on time?"

Abbie waits until she's done chewing and says, "I'm afraid not. We've tweaked everything we could possibly tweak."

"I agree," Marc says. "So, that means that if we want to improve our performance, we need to do something very different than what we are currently doing."

"Makes sense." Abbie shrugs her shoulders. "But different or not, there is nothing I can think of."

"Well, I came across an unconventional approach in one of my MBA classes and I'd like to run it by you."

"That sounds interesting." Abbie is digging into her salad. "Shoot."

Marc opens up a presentation Professor Silver has posted on the student's online board and tilts his computer screen so Abbie can see it. He tells her about running projects with and without bad multitasking and the negative effects it has on setups, rework, and especially on the projects' lead time. He explains the concept of controlling WIP and the idea to start by freezing projects in order to shorten the lead time.

Abbie is listening quietly as she eats. Once Marc is done, Abbie closes the plastic box and puts it aside.

"These are interesting concepts," she says. "They certainly make you think."

"Think about what?" Marc wants to know where her head is.

"Well, let's see." Abbie attempts to organize her thoughts. "For a start, you keep saying 'bad multitasking.' Is there 'good multitasking'?"

Marc recalls someone asking that very question in class. "The professor said that multitasking is good or bad depending on how it affects the overall flow of projects. For example, if A gets stuck in the middle of a project, and B stops what they are doing and helps A out so both of them can quickly move on, the overall flow of projects benefits, so that's good multitasking. But if people constantly go back and forth between projects and the overall flow is much slower, that's bad multitasking."

"I see," Abbie says. "So as long as we don't have a projects' flow speedometer, the whole thing is theoretical. We can't really judge if our multitasking is good or bad."

"Exactly," Marc replies. "That's why the professor said it's useless to go there. Instead, we should be practical. We know we suffer from all the negative consequences of bad multitasking. To rectify it, we should start controlling the WIP."

Abbie takes a minute to digest the new term. "That sure is very different from how we do things now."

Marc can tell Abbie is hesitant. No wonder. "Look at how many late projects we have," he presses. "We are now working on thirty-six projects in parallel. Thirty-six! And I'm desperately talking to angry customers begging them for extensions. It doesn't make sense to go on doing nothing about it."

Abbie pauses and looks at Marc. "This is not a theoretical discussion. You are seriously considering freezing projects."

"Yes, I am," Marc replies.

"Are you for real?" Abbie is astonished. "Why would you risk it?"

There is no way Marc is telling anyone about his father's intention to sell the company, including Abbie. He goes with another angle. "You said earlier that the way we currently operate we already tweaked everything we could possibly tweak. I am committed to finding a better way to manage the engineering department, and this approach has been successfully implemented in many companies."

Abbie is not sure what to think, but she can tell Marc is determined.

"I want to try this," he says, "and I want your help."

Abbie picks up her cellphone and clears the rest of the afternoon. Once she puts her phone down, she looks for something positive to say. "It makes sense that you triaged the projects first and got rid of the low-value projects." Marc agrees. He tells Abbie he heard in class that in some cases the triage uncovered so much lost time and resources that there was hardly any need to freeze additional projects. But this is clearly not the case for them.

"Let's say that you were to give it a try," Abbie is looking for the right words, "how many projects will you freeze?"

"Well, the objective is to shorten our lead time, right?" Marc wants her to follow his reasoning. "What's the shortest project you recall we have ever done?"

Abbie knows what legendary project Marc is referring to. "The H202, a few years ago." It was a rather large project that due to special circumstances they had to finish in record time. "We pulled a miracle and somehow got it done in three months. But that was a huge onetime effort."

"We got it done in three months, which means it's possible. I'd like to get to a point in which we finish every project in three months."

"Let me get this straight." Abbie is alarmed. "Right now our lead time is six months and we barely make it, and you want to cut it by half? How can we possibly do it without considerably reducing the number of projects we deliver?"

"We're not compromising on the throughput," Marc replies. "We are keeping the overall number of projects we deliver the same, and we cut the lead time in half." Marc takes a breath before he finishes the sentence. "I think that means we need to cut the number of projects we work on in parallel, also in half."[5]

"You're thinking of freezing half the projects." Abbie sounds like she is choking. "Seriously?"

Marc takes a minute before he says, "Abbie, we are dangerously close to losing more customers. I want to see if there is something in this approach to managing projects. And to test it, we need to go all in."

Abbie has a distinct feeling there is more to it. But obviously that's all Marc is willing to tell her at this point. She is not sure what to say. "What if this goes wrong?"

"We'll keep a very close eye on the projects. Any sign that things are not working, I need to know about it."

He can tell Abbie is not happy. "Let's give it three months. Right now we commit to six months lead time. To deliver the same number of projects, we should be able to complete the half we keep active in less than three months. Then complete the half we currently freeze in the remaining three months."

Abbie knows Marc is talking in averages, but what he says is reasonable. If it doesn't work, they should know by then.

I should know in a lot less than three months, Marc thinks to himself. If the lead time shrinks like he is hoping, the projects that are closer to completion should finish a lot faster. Or, he'll hear his father is moving forward with selling the company.

They both keep quiet, not sure where to go from here.

After a while Marc says, "Can I show you what I have in mind?"

Abbie reluctantly goes along.

Marc pulls up the projects report file on his screen. "I'm

thinking we should freeze the bottom half, the projects that we need to deliver later on."

Abbie leans forward to get a better look. Marc can smell her subtle perfume.

Finally she says, "I would keep us working on R119 even though it has a later due date."

Marc agrees. This is an important customer. "You're right. We have to ensure we deliver their project on time."

Marc creates a new spreadsheet that now has nineteen projects, including the R119. They spend some time making sure each project manager has between two and three projects. That means a few of the projects need to be reassigned. They also set clear priorities: which projects they need to be working on first and so on. Once they are done, they lean back in their chairs and look at the screen.

Abbie is very uncomfortable about the whole thing. But she is not the one who needs to make the decision.

"Well," she finally says, "if you want me to give it some more thought, I need to sleep on it. But if you have already decided, let me know how I can help."

Marc is wholeheartedly grateful. That's the reason he loves working with Abbie.

"I want to roll it out tomorrow. Will you help me figure out how to explain it to the others?"

They spend the rest of the afternoon planning for tomorrow. All Abbie can think is that she hopes it will work.

10 | The Multitasking Game

The following day at noon, the conference room is full. All the chairs around the table are taken and there are extra chairs all around the walls. The engineers are curious about the reason for the unexpected meeting, but in the meantime they enjoy the good burgers that Marc and Abbie ordered for lunch. Once everyone takes a seat Marc starts off by sincerely thanking everyone for their efforts in the past few months.

"You all did your best and it hasn't gone unnoticed." Marc looks around the room and keeps going. "As hard as we worked, the fact of the matter is that we are behind on too many projects, and we need to do something about it."

"Are you going to ask us to come in regularly on the weekends?" someone asks.

"No." Marc is clear. "We are going to find the needed time within the hours you already put in."

"Good luck with that..." is all he gets.

Noah, the informal leader of the group, says, "I'm so busy you won't find an extra hour in my week to squeeze."

"Well, let me ask you something, Noah. Do you happen to multitask?"

Noah is amused. "I'm the ultimate multitasker! I multitask between projects, between tasks, between keyboard strikes. There is no training in the world that can show me how to multitask more."

"What if you should multitask less?" Marc says. "I think the lost time is in the multitasking."

Marc gets the baffled looks he was hoping for and suggests, "I know it sounds weird. Let me show you. Let's play a little game."

Marc hands each person a piece of paper. Shoot, not everyone has pens and he forgot to bring extra ones. Never mind, they all have their phones with them, he'll improvise.

"Grab your phones and send a text message to Abbie. In that message, you have three projects to complete," Marc explains as he points to the top of the paper.

"Each project has twelve tasks. For the first project, type in capital letters the word M-U-L-T-I-T-A-S-K-I-N-G. In the second, type the numbers one through twelve. And in the third, type the symbols ? [% four times. There's no multitasking here. Complete the projects one by one and as soon as you're done, text it to Abbie."

Complete the Following 3 Projects:

1) M U L T I T A S K I N G

2) 1 2 3 4 5 6 7 8 9 10 11 12

3) ? [% ? [% ? [% ? [%

Some are raising eyebrows, but they are willing to cooperrate. "Are you ready?" Marc asks. He confirms that Abbie has marked the time and says, "Go."

After a minute Abbie's phone starts to ping, and pretty soon she gets text messages from everyone. Abbie says she got the first text after 67 seconds and the last one after 113 seconds.

"Excellent. Now," Marc continues, "let's multitask. You need to perform the same three projects as before, but this time, after you type one letter from the M-U-L-T-I-T-A-S-K-I-N-G project, switch to type one number from the second project, then switch to type one symbol from the third project. Repeat the multitasking until you complete all three projects and then text them to Abbie. Is everyone ready? Go."

Marc can tell they are into it and, as expected, this time it takes longer. After a while Abbie's phone starts pinging, and once she gets the last one, Abbie confirms. She got the first text after 137 seconds and the last one after 256 seconds.

People are mostly quiet. Some are curious how much it took them personally to complete the projects with and without multitasking, so Abbie tells them.

"Interesting," Noah admits. "I'm not sure why, but you're right, Marc. When multitasking, the same projects took the same people a lot more time."

"I know it comes as a surprise," Marc tells him, "but we are losing considerable time when we go back and forth between projects. If we limit our multitasking, we'll be much more efficient. We'll get more done, faster."

Abbie studies her phone. "I can also say that in the multitasking part there were significantly more mistakes."

"Makes sense." Marc is glad she brought it up. "If we reduce the multitasking, we'll likely have fewer quality issues."

"So, you want us to multitask less. But how can we possibly do that under the pressure to make progress on so many projects?" Noah is skeptical.

"You're right, it's pretty much impossible to do with so many projects. That's why I'd like each of you to work only on two or three projects," Marc answers.

"And what about the rest?"

"From now on we'll limit our amount of work in process. As soon as one project is completed, we'll release the next one in line. To get started we'll temporality freeze half of the projects."

Everyone gets talking. The general consensus is that Marc is out of his mind. Marc can hear Linda, their software expert, saying quietly to Noah, "It will never work!"

Noah asks her, "What do you think will happen?"

Linda says, "He will manage to hold it for a couple of weeks tops, and then he'll press us to get going on all the projects he froze."

"I can see that," Noah says to her. "So, why do you care? We thought he was going to ask us to come in to work all weekends right away. Instead, he'll ask for it in a few weeks."

Marc can tell people are not convinced. He says, "Listen, let's give this a try."

Linda interjects. "Marc, with all due respect, do you really think that if a customer calls and says there are issues with the software, you won't ask me to put aside whatever I'm working on and get on it?"

"Good point, Linda." Marc had already discussed this

with Abbie; it's an issue. "This will still be a top priority for you. But no matter what, I won't ask you or anyone else to stop what they are doing if they are in the middle of a task. Most of your tasks are a few hours long and even the most urgent problem can wait for a few hours. You start a task, you complete it."

"What about inquiries from production or integration?" someone asks.

"Good question." Marc is keen to show he'll take some of the load on himself. He also wants to see if something can be done to reduce these interruptions. "Send all of them to me. I'm familiar with all the projects and I'll do my best to handle as many of them as possible. Let's keep the multitasking to a minimum."

People can tell Marc has made up his mind, but they can't imagine he'll be able to control the WIP. Some are against the idea altogether. Others say they might as well enjoy a little time with less stress before the madness returns. Marc is not saying a word.

It takes some time before the room is quiet. Everyone is looking at Marc. "I appreciate your concerns, but this is what we are doing. We all have a lot to gain if we figure out how to reduce the multitasking and shorten the lead times. We are freezing half of the projects starting tomorrow. Most of you work on the most urgent projects anyway so you'll just keep doing what you do, but some of you will get new assignments. I'd like you to stick to your priorities. Work on your number one priority until you're done with it and only then move on to priority number two and so on. In any case, no one works on the projects that are frozen." Marc explains that he will be emailing the updated list of assignments this afternoon.

The meeting is over, and people go back to their desks. They've had their fair share of "flavor of the month changes" before. They are expected to give it a try, but no one really believes it will work.

11 The Misconception about Starting Early

A couple of days later, Marc is doing morning rounds in the engineering department. He is well aware of the power of inertia and he is making sure no one is working on the projects that were frozen.

Marc's cellphone rings. His father in on the line. He wants Marc in his office ASAP.

Isaac heard from one of their customers, who had approved their proposal a couple of months ago, shortly after Doolen left. The customer is deeply worried. His people contacted Wilson with a requested change and heard they are currently not working on the project.

Marc braces himself as he walks to his father's office. This conversation was bound to happen sooner or later. Maybe it's for the best that it's sooner. He isn't comfortable keeping his father in the dark.

Sophia is at her desk outside of his father's office. She gestures to Marc to go right in. His father is waiting for him.

"Talk to me." Isaac is all business.

Marc tries to slow things down. "We all want the same

thing," he starts. "We want to meet the due dates. This is why when we received a new project, we immediately put it into work. We assumed that the sooner we start working on it the greater the chance we'll get it done in time."

"Correct."

"Not so fast," Marc replies. "Starting early with all the projects means we have more of them in WIP. The more projects we work on, the more time we waste going back and forth between them. Starting early with each project does not increase its chances of being completed on time. Rather, it jeopardizes the chances of any of the projects being completed on time."

Isaac takes a minute to think about it.

Marc continues. "I want to get to a point where we have fewer projects in WIP at any point in time. This will reduce the multitasking and ensure we get them in and out much faster. That way we get what we wished for, we shorten the lead time, and we meet the deadlines."

"Go on."

"The only thing is, to get started I needed to get some of the load off the engineers, so I temporarily froze some of the projects that are due for later on."

"I see."

It appears his father may be willing to listen, so Marc goes into details. When he's done, he adds, "This is a much better way to manage the flow of projects. Think about it: to start early, we assigned a project to a project manager as soon as we got it, and if that project manager got delayed with one of his previous projects, the new one didn't get much work done on it, sometimes until it was too late. Now, I'll keep the projects in one central list. As soon as one of the project managers completes a project, I will assign them the next one on the list. That way the load is better spread among the project managers."

It's common sense. Isaac is impressed. It might be what he's been looking for all these years; the effective way to manage engineering. Isaac taps with his fingers on the desk. He made the tough decision to sell the company because he didn't see another way out, but Marc believes that he has found such a way. If Marc succeeds it will get them out of the ditch, but even though Marc is enthusiastic, his chances of success are slim. Isaac wishes Marc had come across it a couple of years ago. He would have loved to try it with him. But changes of this magnitude take considerable time to figure out and many of them don't bring the desired results. This one is particularly risky; if the lead time won't shrink fast enough, they may jeopardize the projects that are currently frozen. They could fall flat on their faces before Marc figures it out. Isaac wishes they had more time, but time is the one thing he doesn't have.

The only sound in the room is the tapping of Isaac's fingers. He needs to make up his mind. Refusing to let Marc pursue his initiative is the wrong way to go. Isaac doesn't want to ruin the good relationship he has with his son. He also doesn't want Marc to get up and leave. Isaac decides he won't stop Marc from trying this new way of managing his department, for now. He'll give Marc some space, but he won't stop pursuing his plan to sell, either.

"This is a bold move, son," Isaac says, and continues in a stern voice, "don't mess up. I'm meeting with Laramie's people next week."

Laramie is one of the rapidly growing companies in their industry and everyone knows about their recent purchasing spree. Marc is not happy to hear that at all. But he has his father's consent to go on for now. At this point that's all he can hope for. He crosses his fingers under the desk and promises his father he knows what he's doing.

––––––––––––

Marc goes back to finish his rounds in the department, then he heads to his office. He barely sits down when his cellphone rings. It's his sister. Just what he needs right now.

"Marc, what the hell! Third order for production in a week, again?! Either you're late on the dates that you commit to, or you finish three projects in one week?! What do you think I am, a magician? Where will I get the capacity to produce the parts for three projects at the same time?! How many times do I have to tell you..."

Sam keeps yelling but Marc isn't listening anymore. Finish three projects in one week, he is thinking. Where did he see this lately?

Marc puts his cellphone on his desk. Sam is going to yell for a while, but he doesn't have to take it. He opens Professor Silver's presentation and searches for the bad multitasking illustration. He looks at the rows of rectangles and squares on screen. There it is. In the bottom row, when multitasking, all the projects finish close together. Is it possible that multitasking also contributes to the fluctuation in the workload down the line? It probably does. If they go back and forth between the projects, working on all of them at the same time, it's not surprising that they also finish them around the same time. And this results in fluctuations in production–there are times when they are waiting for us and times when they are flooded. And of course integration keeps pressing them to deliver. Marc recalls the time when he managed the integration department. They were constantly complaining about the peaks and delays in the workload. It appears that it all starts in engineering. The multitasking in engineering is not only a killer of time for them, it's also a killer of capacity for the departments down the line. No wonder his sister has had it with them.

But, if this is the case, then controlling WIP, working on far fewer projects at a time, and starting a new project only once a previous one is completed, should also solve this issue.

Right?

"Hello, Marc, are you there? Are you listening to me?"

Marc picks up the phone and says, "I'm sorry, Sam. I believe I have found a way to avoid these peaks from now on. I'm trying something new here."

"You better!"

For the second time in an hour, Marc crosses his fingers and promises he knows what he is doing.

12 | Dynamics of Theories and Trends

The following week, it's late on Friday afternoon. Marc is getting ready to leave when Abbie shows up at the door to his office. "Do you have a minute?"

"What's up?"

"We may have a mutiny in the making." Abbie tells Marc that a couple of project managers have started talking about going back to work on projects that were frozen. They have nothing to work on, and more people are considering joining them.

"What about the projects they are supposed to be working on?"

Abbie is not sure.

Marc asks her to look into it before he makes any rash decisions. He has to leave soon as he has plans for the evening.

An hour later Marc is sitting in an elegant restaurant. The table is covered with a crisp, white tablecloth and is set for two. Marc hopes his date is not going to be late. He's hungry.

Tim, his gym buddy, has persuaded him to go out with his neighbor.

"She's cool," Tim promised him, "I'd date her if I wasn't married."

A tall, thin woman enters the main room and looks around. Marc only had time for a quick glance at her social media picture, but this is surely her. He stands up and she notices him and smiles. As she is walking toward their table, Marc takes the opportunity to study her. Not gorgeous but definitely cool, he concludes. Tim was right.

"Hi, I'm Tina," she introduces herself.

"I'm Marc." A handshake seems too businesslike. He offers a light hug, which she accepts.

As they review the menu, Marc is glad to hear she'll join him for wine. "Is Merlot okay?"

"Sure." Tina is game. "I like red wine with my steak."

Marc is relieved. Too many blind dates ended right there, when his date wasn't into any alcohol or was on one of those extreme diets where all she would eat is a salad with no dressing.

The sommelier arrives with their wine and goes through the ceremony of opening the bottle and pouring Marc a taste. The wine is good. Marc approves and the sommelier fills their glasses.

As they are waiting for their food, Marc learns Tina is an architect and an interior designer. She works for one of the known firms in town and focuses mainly on private houses.

"What about you?" Tina asks.

Marc has no desire to talk about work, so he chooses to

tell her about his Executive MBA program. "We review a wide range of management theories. Most are classic, some are trendy."

Marc tells her that he finds it interesting that some major management theories fade away and others are around for a long time even if they are not widely accepted.

Tina is aware of the dynamics of trends and theories in her field. "Some trends become part of the norm so they are not considered trends anymore," she says, "and some trends shouldn't have been born in the first place."

"Like what?"

"Like glass kitchen counters. They were in all the magazines and high-end exhibitions for a little while, and thank God they went away."

"So what's the current trend?" Marc is looking to keep the conversation going.

"Well," Tina is thinking, "the open space in the kitchen and living room has been the way to go for a while, and now they are trying to move this concept into the master bedroom and unite it with the bathroom.

"I can see the appeal for newlyweds..." Marc smiles with a wink.

"Yeah, the question is will they still like it when the honeymoon phase is over," Tina laughs.

The waitress clears their plates and asks about desserts. They both prefer to just finish their wine.

It had turned out to be a very pleasant evening. Marc takes the last sip from his glass of wine thinking, *I wish we could have another bottle over at my place.*

He realizes he was talking out loud when Tina smiles and says, "I'm in."

13 Full-kit

The next morning, after his workout, Marc takes a quick shower at the gym so he won't be late to class. As he gets his phone out of the locker, he notices an email from Abbie. Noah, who had started the mutiny, had nothing to do. He can't work on his top priority project because he is missing some final requirements. When they started working on this model, they had sent an inquiry about these requirements to the customer and moved on. Now Noah found out that they had never heard back from the customer. Going back and forth between many projects, it was easy for details like this to slip through the cracks. Noah can't work on his second project because something else is missing. So he wants to go back to work on his previous project, which was frozen.

———

With no homework to review, Rick starts the lecture differently. "Last time we discussed the rule of flow for controlling WIP. Any questions?"

Kiara says they are looking into the option of implementing it in the IT division, and they can already tell that freezing projects won't stop a lot of the day-to-day multitasking. Managers from other departments are so used to interrupting the IT people whenever they need something, that it is bound to be an issue. It seems like multitasking is in their culture.

Shonda says that in their marketing department they are thinking about instituting "Saturday hours" as part of the regular workday.

She explains. "You would expect the office to be empty on Saturdays, but in fact it's not. Some people found that the constant interruptions made it impossible for them to work during the week. So they come in for a few hours on Saturday to complete their tasks."

Shonda continues, "You should see them on a Saturday. They don't chat with anyone. They don't read emails. They don't answer their phones. They put their heads down and get their job done."

"I see," Kiara says. "You're thinking about having mandatory 'no interruptions' hours during the day."

Marc says they had another idea. "After we froze projects, I was expecting the multitasking to go to a minimum, but I soon realized that people continued to constantly consult with each other. It's enough that an engineer is distracted just a few times to answer questions from his buddies, and each time it takes only twenty, twenty-five minutes before they go back to their work, but by then the morning is pretty much ruined."

Marc tells the class that to raise people's awareness, he

introduced the pizza donations jar. Each time they interrupt someone when that other person is in the middle of a task, they need to donate a dollar to the pizza jar. "When the jar gets full, we buy pizza for everyone for the next lunch. We had pizza for lunch almost every day for the first few days, but now people have gotten the point and there are way fewer interruptions."

Rick wants to make sure he heard right. "You already froze projects? How many did you freeze?"

Marc says, "Fifty percent."

Rick is impressed. Marc doesn't talk much in class and Rick had no idea he was that serious.

"And how is it working so far?" Rick asks.

"Actually, I think we may have frozen too many projects." Marc tells the class about the issue Noah ran into.

Rick is not surprised. "You need a full-kit."

Marc is not familiar with the term.

"Let me explain," Rick says, and turns to the class.

"One of the notorious obstacles to flow is the need to frequently stop because we are missing something that is essential in order to move forward. 'Full-kit' means that before we start a task or a project, we first verify we have everything we need to complete it."

This is a key concept, so Rick wants to make sure everyone gets it. "Let me show you what I mean. Let's say you want to paint a room in your house. Take a couple of minutes and write down the full-kit, the list of all the things you'll need to prepare before getting started."

The students play along and someone volunteers to write his list on the whiteboard.

Full-Kit for Painting a Room

Paint tray	Painter's tape
Wall paint (satin/grey, 2 gallons)	Drop cloths
Trim paint (semi-gloss, white, 1 gallon)	Step ladder
Ceiling paint (flat, white, 1 gallon)	Roller frame
Stirring sticks	Roller nap (1/2")
Cleaning rags	Extension pole
2" angled paint brush	

Rick says, "I can see there is paint in here, and rollers, and tape and other stuff. Is that a full-kit?"

"No," Marc says. "If you want to do a good job painting the room, you also need a screwdriver, some kind of filler, a putty knife, and sandpaper."

"Excellent," Rick affirms, "that is precisely the point. You can get all the items on the list ready and as soon as you start to work, you have to stop because you didn't get the materials needed to take care of the screws and nails in the walls."

Rick adds the items that Marc mentioned to the list on the whiteboard and asks, "Is that a full-kit?"

"It depends. The quantities of paints you'll need depends on the size of the room. Charlie is on a roll. "You'll also need a primer if the room was previously painted in a darker color, and if it was previously covered with wallpaper you'll need stuff to remove it, and..."

"That's an important point." Rick gestures to Charlie that he can stop. "Every project is somewhat different and its full-kit should be detailed in accordance."

Rick looks at the whiteboard and realizes he should make another point. "The full-kit needs to contain everything that is required. Not just the physical items."

"I was just thinking about that," Shonda says. "If my husband plans to paint a room without getting my approval for the color, God help him."

"Right," Kiara says. "And if my husband plans to paint a room without getting a professional to do it, God help all of us."

Everyone laughs.

"Approvals and resources are key items in many full-kits," Rick agrees. "The full-kit is a checklist that contains all the elements that are necessary to complete a task or a project."

Shonda says, "And you don't start working until you verify that all the boxes in the full-kit are checked."

"That makes sense," Kiara says. "Why would we start working on a project just to stop a little later? Then we move to the next project and the next one, and it's a recipe for having too many incomplete projects and bad multitasking."

Marc can speak from experience. "With too many open projects, and the option to always move to another one, we are bound to forget to follow up and ensure we get whatever was missing."

Rick says, "The full-kit is essential to support controlling the WIP."

Marc gets it. Full-kit is the key. Without it his people are bound to waste the valuable time they gained by freezing the projects.

Rick moves on. "What are your thoughts about a full-kit that is not in writing?"

Shonda doesn't hesitate. "It's useless. I can tell you for a fact that if the list is not in writing we are bound to forget some items."

Rick smiles. There's little doubt that Shonda is an avid lists user. "That's right. And who should be in charge of full-kitting?

"An expert," Shonda replies. "Someone with profound understanding of the subject, who knows the specific details required to complete the project."

Rick nods. "What do you think will happen if the professional that Kiara's husband hires decides he doesn't have time to full-kit before he starts painting their house and delegates that assignment to his new helper?"

"It's very likely that the project will come to a halt because essential things will be missing." Kiara sounds like she is speaking from experience.

Rick says, "In every project there is uncertainty, so we know we can't always predict everything that we may need. But, to maximize the chances that the project won't suffer from delays, the experts are the ones who should be in charge of full-kitting. This is a much better use of their time than firefighting emergencies caused by missing things."

"How do you determine where you need a full-kit?" comes a question from the corner. Ted has been quiet until now.

This is an excellent question. Rick is almost sorry it was Ted who asked it. "Well, you need to look at your operation and identify all the junctions in which major tasks start; junctions in which there is a synchronization between re-

sources or there is a handover of the work to the next resource in line. In each of these junctions there should be
a gate. When a task or project arrives at the gate, the gate
should be closed. The next resource in line will not be per-
mitted to start working on that task or project before we
verify it has a full-kit."

"So, the first gate should be at the starting point of the
projects, and additional gates should be established down
the line, as needed?" Shonda wants to make sure she understands.

"Correct. The initial effort is to identify where in the operation you should have gates. Then you need to appoint
someone to be responsible for watching the gates. Each
time a task or project arrives at a gate, the gatekeeper will
check that it has a full-kit and only then open the gate, al-
lowing work to continue."

"And you only got around to talking about this now?"
Ted mutters. "You could have saved me a lot of grief if you
just started the course with this."

Rick puts his tongue at the roof of his mouth so he can't
speak. His mother taught him that many years ago.

"Come on, Ted," Marc says. "Professor Silver said at the
very beginning that different rules of flow are more relevant
to different environments."

Shonda has less patience than Marc. "With all due respect, Ted, for you it might be better to start with implementing a full-kit but for others it will be a waste of time to
get full-kits for projects that are going to be canceled during
the triage."

"Or spend valuable time preparing full-kits for projects
that are going to be frozen for a while when starting to con-

trol the WIP," says someone else.

Ted keeps quiet. He needs to back off.

Rick wants to make sure he gives them their homework early this time. "Here is what I'd like you to do for our next class. Examine your operation and determine where you should have gates. In each gate, decide who is the right person, or people, to be in charge of full-kitting, and who should be the gatekeeper. Describe the process of opening the gate; the process of verifying the full-kit and confirming the next task can start. At last, as an example, choose one project and write down all the full-kits it will need at the various gates."

A murmur of protest runs through the class.

"This is a lot of work!"

"We need more time!"

"Fine," Rick says. He is OK with them submitting their homework for the class after next. Anyway, he had invited a guest for the next class.

There is plenty of time for questions and the students have lots of them.

It's already dark when Marc drives home from the university. He is eager to tell Abbie about the full-kit, but it's not really appropriate to call on a Saturday night.

Abbie picks up on the third ring. "Hi Marc, is everything okay?"

It feels nice to hear her voice. "Yeah, I just wanted to tell you I know how put a stop to the mutiny. Do you have a minute?"

"That's great!" Abbie sounds like she is in a bit of a hurry. "Can it wait until Monday? Someone is picking me up soon and I have to get ready."

Full retreat. "No worries, enjoy your date."

Abbie doesn't deny it. "Thanks!"

14 | T Minus Preparation

On Monday morning, Marc gathers all the project managers in the conference room. He wants to make sure each of the projects has a full-kit so the engineers can continue working.

"Remember the last time we were here, I wanted to demonstrate the effect of multitasking?" he starts. "I came up with the three 'projects' and the instructions to complete them with and without multitasking. I wrote the instructions down and printed enough copies. I made sure Abbie was ready to mark the time, but I forgot to bring enough pens for everyone."

"Yeah," Abbie smiles, "that was a good save when you asked everyone to use their phones."

Marc appreciates the kind words, but that's not the point. "The point is, I needed that save because I didn't make sure to have a full-kit."

Marc explains the concept and suggests they practice by writing down the full-kits that were required to start working on their top priority projects. It doesn't take long to do and not surprisingly the lists are pretty similar. They contain all the customer's requirements, budget, regulatory and industry standards they need to follow, deliverables from the customers that were agreed upon, and a few other items depending on whether they need to build a prototype for the project or not.

"What I'd like you to do as soon as you go back to your desk is verify that you have a full-kit for all your active projects. If you're missing something, let me know. Then, those of you who can continue to work on your top priority, go back to work. Those of you who are stuck please join me and we'll do whatever it takes to prepare all the full-kits as soon as possible.

Noah asks, "What about the next projects and the ones after that?"

"Good question." Marc is ready. "Think of the entry point to our operation as having a physical gate. From now on, we will open the gate and start working on the next project only if it has a full-kit."

Noah asks, "Can you guarantee that you'll tell us enough time in advance what our next project will be, so that we can arrange for a full-kit to be ready in time?"

Marc recalls Professor Silver calling it "T-Preparation" in class. "How much time in advance, before you start working on a project, do you need to start preparing its full-kit?"

It doesn't a take long discussion to figure out the process.

"For this to work, we need to be meticulous," Marc clarifies. "I will be guarding the gate and I will be expecting a full-kit every time."

Noah is not alarmed. "No one here likes wasting their time. Just be sure to let us know about our next assignment enough time in advance, like we just agreed."

The meeting ends and Marc spends the rest of the day assisting the project managers in getting what is missing. When emails will not do, they get on the phone.

Later in the afternoon, Marc is on his computer when Abbie enters his office with coffee and a couple of sandwiches. Marc realizes how hungry he is. No wonder, he was too busy to have lunch. He invites Abbie to come in and gratefully takes the sandwich that she hands him. They didn't have a chance to talk since the brief phone call on Saturday night.

"So, what do you think?" Marc asks as they unwrap the sandwiches.

"About the mutiny?" she smiles. "The battle is averted. How do we ensure people won't end up without a full-kit again?"

"Let me show you." Marc tilts his computer screen so Abbie can see what he was doing. It is a WIP board that contains all the projects they are currently working on.

The WIP board has five columns and a row for each of the project managers. The second column is entitled On Deck. "These are the projects that are next in line," Marc explains. "As soon as I pull a project into this column, I assign it to a project manager and let them know they need to start preparing its full-kit."

The Engineering WIP Board

P.Manager	On Deck	WIP	On Hold	Completed
1) Noah	▨ ▨	▨	▨ ▨	
2) Abbie	▨ ▨	▨ ▨	▨	
3) ...	▨ ▨	▨	▨ ▨	
4) ...	▨ ▨	▨ ▨ ▨		
5) ...	▨	▨ ▨	▨	
6) ...	▨	▨ ▨	▨	
7) Linda	▨	▨		

"I see," Abbie says and looks at the third column, which is entitled WIP. She recognizes the projects. "These are the projects that we are currently working on."

"Right," Marc confirms. "Our gate is between the On Deck column and the WIP column. Before I pull a project into WIP, I'll verify with the assigned project manager that he prepared a full-kit."

Marc points to the fourth column. "I named this one On Hold. Right now, it has quite a few projects because we just got started with the full-kit. In the future, I hope to see this column as empty as possible. Whenever someone gets stuck, I want to know about it right away and get the project back into the WIP column as soon as possible."

Abbie is impressed. "That's wise. If a project gets into the On Hold column for a random reason, you take care of it and move on. But if you find that projects keep getting stuck for the same reason, that means we should have taken care of it beforehand."

"Precisely. So we'll add it to our full-kit."

Abbie looks back at the WIP board. "And obviously the last column is Completed."

"Having considerably fewer projects in the flow provides clarity we didn't have before," Marc says, "and the WIP board will enable me to see the full picture, control the WIP, and ensure full-kit compliance at the gate."

"I like it," Abbie says. "I may create my own WIP board if you don't mind."

"Absolutely. The WIP board is particularly useful at the task level. Especially since, as our mechanical expert, you are involved in many of the other projects."

Abbie can see that. "I'll incorporate my tasks from the projects that I'm managing, plus the tasks for the other projects that need my assistance."

Marc smiles. "I intend to clear the last column every month, but I bet you'll never take any item off it."

Abbie smiles back. "That's me all right. I'll enjoy watching the completed tasks piling up."

"Speaking of enjoying," Marc treads lightly, "sorry for interrupting you on Saturday night. I hope you had a good time."

"Oh dear." Abbie shakes her head at the memory. "A dreadful blind date. I used the first opportunity to bail."

15 Enough Weight, Enough Repetitions

Early in the morning, Marc enters the gym and spots his buddy Tim. They both have years of experience in strength training and are used to training together. A novice may think it's about doing a little bit of everything in order to cover all the muscles in every workout. But proper training is very different. The idea is to work on fewer groups of muscles in each session but do enough weight and enough repetitions to properly exhaust the muscles and build their strength. At the same time you allow the muscles you worked on last time adequate rest and recovery.

Marc and Tim finish warming up and proceed to follow their upper-body routine. Tim starts his bench presses and Marc stands next to him, ready to assist.

"Two more," Marc says as Tim is getting close to finishing his first set. He spots Tim in his last press, and then helps him lift the bar back in its place.

Tim takes a minute to rest before his next set. "How is it going with Tina?"

"We went out a couple more times."

"And?"

"And she is not the one."

"I thought she would check all the boxes," Tim says.

"I guess on paper she does," Marc agrees. "But it's not about checking boxes."

Tim finishes his set, and they switch places. Marc adjusts the weights on the bar. He uses more weight, so he needs fewer repetitions to exhaust his chest muscles.

Next, they pick up dumbbells from the stand and sit on nearby benches to start their shoulder presses.

"So, where do single men meet women these days?" Tim is making conversation.

"Everyone is using dating apps," Marc says, stating the obvious. "But personally, I think these apps do more harm than good. They appear to be helpful, because they provide endless potential partners. But what they actually do is get people used to canceling potential partners. It's just too easy to move to the next one."

"I can see that," Tim says. "So, what's another option?"

"You tell me." Marc starts another set of presses.

"I can tell you what's not an option," Tim says. "Dating someone from work. Too many bad things can happen."

"You're right." Marc dismisses a hint of a thought about Abbie. He knows exactly what Tim is talking about. "Dating someone you work with is not an option."

16 | Dosage

Rick enters the classroom along with a couple of guests. He invites them to take a seat in the front row and starts the lecture. "Today, we'll cover another obstacle to flow that is called dosage. This one is not as common as bad multitasking or lack of full-kit, but when it is obstructing the flow, handling it can make a big difference."

"Dosage?" Kiara is not sure she got the term right.

"Yes. It's what it sounds like. It's about the quantity of work. It relates to project environments in which we attempt to take care of too many projects at the same time and, as a result, we end up paying too little attention to each project. If the dosage is too small, our work is very inefficient, the projects clog the flow, and we get poor results. Therefore, to improve the flow and the quality of our outcome, we need to go deeper and provide a larger dosage of work to each project before we move on to the next one."

Rick stops when he sees the puzzled looks on the students' faces. "Instead of speaking in theoretical terms, let me introduce you to a former student of mine, Bill Meyers. Bill is a top manager at a local aviation company. A couple of years ago, he oversaw the implementation of dosage in their aircraft maintenance operation and he was kind enough to join us today to tell us about it."

Bill stands up and thanks Rick for inviting him. "Hello everyone. You are probably familiar with the aviation world as passengers, and are aware of the times when flights are delayed or canceled due to maintenance issues. But I wonder how many of you are familiar with the mammoth efforts that take place behind the scenes to ensure that the airplanes are well maintained."

"It sure feels like there is room for improvement..." someone comments.

"Always," Bill concurs, and continues. "Passengers' safety is our top priority and as such we take aircraft maintenance very seriously. Our operation takes care of all the planned maintenance, plus the nonroutine issues flagged by the pilots or the ground crew, and these are sometimes urgent, especially if the airplane is being held at the gate. I don't have to tell you that airplanes are very complicated machines with dozens of systems and thousands of parts. The problem was that at any given time, most airplanes had some expiring tasks."

Bill pauses to explain. "Expiring tasks refer to the inspections and checks that need to be done to all these systems and parts every fixed period of time or after a certain amount of flight hours."

It seems people are with him, so Bill continues. "Since at any given time, most airplanes had some expiring tasks, we had to work on almost all the airplanes every day. That was a huge effort that was being further complicated by the fact that often we didn't have the parts or the specialized technicians at the same airport where the airplane was.

"With so much work to get done, and bear in mind that diagnosing and fixing often takes longer than expected, our capacity was spread thin across many airplanes and the technicians were constantly multitasking, rushing from plane to plane, troubleshooting, moving resources, managing towing, and coordinating with planning, central maintenance, et cetera.

"We are under pressure to release the planes as soon as possible since we have to keep the period of time in which the airplane is on the ground to a minimum. So, we ended up performing just the urgent, most essential work. Which further explains why at any given time, most airplanes had some expiring tasks, so we had to work on almost all the planes every day."

Bill takes a breath and continues, "After learning about dosage in class, I started wondering if too little dosage might have been what was causing our maintenance issues. We teamed with a consulting company that specializes in implementing the Theory of Constraints rules of flow, and as I expected, dosage is a key part of our implementation."

Rick can see everyone in the class is interested. "Can you give us more details?"

"By all means." Bill smiles. "The routine things like checking tire air pressure and going through the cabin are still done daily as part of the overnight maintenance. The major change revolves around the bulk of the work, the expiring tasks. We switched from touching every aircraft every day to every couple of weeks. Now, each time we touch an airplane we give it a much bigger dosage of work than before; we check deeper and fix and replace things that are more than just the minimum. We call it 'deep cleaning'. Now we are able to schedule maintenance much better and perform most of it at our maintenance centers. The emergencies are a lot fewer and farther apart, and the flow is much better."

"Provided that you have full-kits." Rick gets the picture.

"You bet." Bill couldn't agree more. "We require full preparation of parts, work packages, technicians, documents, troubleshooting history, et cetera for each scheduled aircraft. Full-kit is so important that we incorporated it into our new set of measurements."

"A new set of measurements?" Shonda is interested.

"I won't go into the details of our new operational performance and flexibility measurements, but I will tell you that our maintenance performance measurements now include the number of aircrafts in WIP as well as full-kit compliance."

Charlie is curious. "What would you say was your biggest hurdle in this implementation?"

Bill takes a minute to think. "I would say that the toughest one to overcome was to convince the maintenance staff to go along. All they could see was that we were asking them to do more work. Which, in a way, we were."

Charlie admits he doesn't get it.

Bill smiles. "Think about it. Providing a larger dosage for each aircraft means that we perform not only the tasks that are currently expired, but also tasks that will expire in the next two weeks. If, for example, an aircraft arrives and its brakes need inspection next week, we'll go ahead and take care of it right away. Inspection for brakes is done every X amount of landings, which means the next brakes maintenance will have to be done earlier and so forth. So, if you focus on the local optimum, you look only at the maintenance of brakes, the technicians are in fact doing more work on it per year. But if you look at the big picture, the global optimum, since we maintain the brakes as part of a deep cleaning of other systems, we touch this airplane a lot fewer times, we multitask considerably less between airplanes, we seldom have to fly technicians or parts to maintain airplanes in airports in the middle of nowhere. Our overall flow is better by far."

Kiara says, "That sure is counterintuitive."

Bill agrees. "This implementation included some major changes, but I would say that the biggest change was in our perception. We used to think that maximizing the efficiency of each resource, technician, or work station would yield the best global results. But now we know that local efficiency does not translate into global efficiency. Our primary objective is to maximize the flow."

After Bill answers a few more questions Rick stands up and turns to the class. "I hope you have a better understanding now of what dosage means."

Marc thinks about it. It looks complicated when they are talking about the maintenance of a fleet of airplanes, but the concept of dosage is pretty simple. This is exactly what they are doing at the gym by limiting each workout to fewer muscle groups and using enough weight and repetitions.

Rick explains, "Dosage is basically another form of controlling WIP. When we increase the dosage to the right level, it usually means we reduce the number of projects we work on in parallel, so we are actually reducing the bad multitasking."

Bill interjects, "Professor Silver, if you don't mind, before you go into the theory, we'd like to share another implementation." He points to the woman who came in with him. "By all means." Rick is surprised. When Bill introduced them earlier, he got the impression that Bill's wife merely came along to keep him company.

"Sandra, will you take it from here?" Sandra Meyers works in their state's Department of Corrections. She is the deputy director in charge of their adult probation and parole division.

Sandra takes Bill's place in front of the class and starts with an overview. "In our rehabilitation programs, we have a duty to ensure the public safety as well as do whatever we can to help the offenders placed under our supervision stay out of trouble and rebuild their lives. These people are either dangerously close to going to jail or just got out and are struggling to get used to life outside. They typically have a hard time reconnecting with family members, finding a stable housing, and getting a steady job. Given that we have a very limited staff, each of our correctional officers had around sixty cases at any given time. Traditionally, the assumption was that we should supervise the offenders for a long period of time to ensure they didn't slip. Each offender got personal one-hour visits every other week for a period of up to a year."

Everyone is listening. Sandra goes on. "The correctional officers, or caseworkers, as we call them, complained all the time about how short these visits were. They said that by the time they managed to fill in the mandatory paperwork their hour was almost up. We had very limited success, but we couldn't do much about it, as we had to attend to all the offenders and there was no way we'd get additional budget for more caseworkers."

Sandra gestures to her husband. "When I heard about the concept of dosage from Bill, it rang a bell. I started wondering if perhaps we suffered from a similar problem: providing too little dosage to too many offenders. But people are not aircraft and I wasn't at all sure that this could work."

"How can you tell what the right dosage should be?" Shonda wonders aloud.

Sandra replies, "That is exactly what I was asking myself. I got together with my team and we tried to estimate how much time we needed to spend with each offender in order to have a real chance at helping them get on track. The first thing that we realized was that we should concentrate our efforts on the first three months of supervision, since this is the critical period when they struggle the most. The second thing we realized was much harder to swallow. It seems that to make a difference we needed to spend with each offender closer to a hundred hours."

"Wow!" Rick is amazed. "Going from one hour every other week for a year to a hundred hours in three months is a pretty large increase in the dosage."

"It's often more than that," Sandra says. "If the court mandates a year's supervision we have to comply with it. The added dosage in the first three months would have to be on top of that."

Everyone is quiet, wondering where this is going.

Sandra continues. "Our first reaction was that this was not doable. But we kept playing with the idea and eventually we came up with the plan for a hundred hours of structured activities. We switched most of the personal meetings in the first three months to group meetings so we could see each offender at least four times a week. In addition, each offender is given assignments they have to perform and report back on. For example, if we get them a job interview, the interview time would count as part of the one hundred hours."

"Can you tell if this is working?" Charlie wants to know.

"Well, a little over a year since we started, the feedback from both the caseworkers and the offenders is very positive. I can tell you that we are already starting to see a reduction the number of parole violations. For most of our other statistics it's too early, but we expect them to reflect positive results as well."

Sandra turns to Rick and says, "And it all started when Bill told me what he learned in your class about dosage. That's why I wanted to come here today and thank you in person."

Rick genuinely appreciates the gesture. These are extraordinary case studies, and he would love to hear more. The students already have their homework for next class, so they can continue. "Any other questions for Bill or Sandra?"

17 | Full-kit Before Production

It's midmorning the following week. Marc is in his office reviewing the WIP board on his computer screen and ensuring the amount of WIP is under control. There is constant pressure to start working on more projects and it's easy to slip and let the number of projects they work on in parallel go up.

Marc is pleased. Everyone has their assigned priorities; they know what to work on and what is next in line. The On Hold column still has more projects than he cares to see, but all of them were reviewed and not surprisingly, in most cases something was missing from their full-kit. Having a full-kit ready before they start working on a project will make a big difference. These preparations are tedious and they take time, but Marc made it clear he would not tolerate any exceptions.

Although they are still under pressure to deliver some urgent projects, the vibe in the department seems different. There are still a lot of interruptions, but overall it's quieter and less hectic than before. There is considerably less multitasking and people are able to concentrate and get their job done. They are completing a bulk of projects that were in the final stages and people are in high spirits. That also goes a long way in getting those who were against the freeze on board.

His cellphone rings. Marc picks it up and sighs. It's his sister.

Production needs to make a special effort to handle the temporary wave of completed projects before the flow will become steady. He has already explained the situation to Sam and thought they were on the same page.

"This is Marc," he answers formally, and holds the phone inches away from his ear.

"Marc, what the hell! We have to get going on the H355s, and my people are stuck because of you! Just look at the drawings for crying out loud! Your people are asking for features that we can't produce, again! I'm under such pressure here and you keep messing up! How many times do I need to tell you..."

When Marc is finally able to get a word in, he finds out what's wrong in the drawings and promises to send the amendments right away.

As much as he doesn't appreciate her tone of voice, his sister is right, again. Marc has noticed how his perception has changed since he started thinking in terms of flow. He had missed an important gate: the handover from engineering to production. This is exactly what Professor Silver was talking about when he cautioned them to look at the whole operation and whenever a project moves to the next hands, there is a need to verify a full-kit.

He looks up H355. It was one of Abbie's projects and it's a complicated one. Marc can't bring himself to be mad at her. Without a full-kit to production and with so much going on, these mishaps are bound to happen from time to time. He better not mess with it. Marc emails Abbie the urgent request. On second thought, he also wants to talk with her.

Abbie answers the phone right away. "Marc, I got your email. Let me take care of it and get back to you."

A few hours later, Abbie enters his office. Marc wonders what took her so long.

"Is everything okay with the H355?" he asks.

"Yes, it required some thinking but production should be able to get going now." Abbie takes a seat and says, "I also took some time to put together a draft for the new full-kit."

Marc guesses, "For the transfer to production?"

"Yes. I reviewed what we sent production in a few recent projects, and I also looked into complaint emails that we got from them in the past. The details for the full-kit for production are in your email."

Marc turns to his computer and reviews the email. He can't think of anything to add to it. Abbie did a good job.

Abbie asks, "How do you suggest we prepare this full-kit for each project?"

Marc takes a minute to think. "Well, the best way to go about it is to have planned handover meetings with the relevant people from engineering and production, as well as Rebecca."

Too often production is stuck because a vendor didn't deliver parts on time and they didn't have enough in inventory. So Rebecca who is in charge of inventory, should definitely take part in these meetings.

Mark adds, "They can review the drawings together and make sure that everything is feasible not only from the production point of view, but also inventory."

Abbie is not overly pleased. "I was hoping you'd think of another way."

Marc can see the value in such meetings. When they transfer projects to production, there's often a lot of turmoil around it with emails, phone calls, and yelling in all directions. Sorting out these final details gets on everyone's nerves and such review meetings will prevent it. "I thought you'd be on board. It will save us a lot of interruptions like the one we just had with the H355. It will turn the chaotic multitasking in the transfer into planned reviews."

"I agree," Abbie says. "It's just that I'm already involved in so many meetings that I hardly have time to work." Everyone complains about spending too much time in meetings, not just Abbie. To make sure that the robotic arms will function properly, they need to see to it that nothing is overlooked, so all the little details in the various steps of development have to be signed off in endless status report meetings. Abbie, as their mechanical expert, is involved in many of them. No wonder that she is not too happy about committing to more planned meetings.

He says, "Thank God the status reports meetings were cut by half when we started controlling the WIP."

"That was a relief, and I do see the benefits in having such full-kit review meetings." Abbie shrugs. "For lack of a better idea, I say let's try it."

Marc moves on. "How do you suggest we make sure

these meetings don't go by the wayside after a while?"

Abbie considers, "I guess only production can tell if they have everything they need, so someone from their side will have to review the drawings before they get started. But you can easily ensure these meetings don't evaporate over time. Simply get alerts whenever we post the meetings' notes on the collaborative tool."

Marc knows what that means. "And follow up, only forever."

Marc thinks about it. If he can make it a habit to post a good word when he sees these notes, his people will know he is watching. People love a pat on the back. He should make a point to praise them for doing a good job, not only intervene when they mess up. Ensuring full-kit compliance this way is a much better use of his time than answering urgent calls from production, which he signed up for when they first discussed controlling WIP.

He turns to Abbie. "We should start these meetings right away. I'll discuss it with Sam and once she approves, we'll get everyone else in the loop."

Abbie leans back in her chair. "So, we started with one gate and ended up with two."

Marc shifts his thoughts back to the gates. "Actually, I think it might be beneficial to have one more."

18 | Additional Gates

The following Sunday, Marc arrives at his parents' house for lunch.

"We're in here," his mother calls when she hears him at the door.

Marc follows her voice into the kitchen.

"I'm so glad you came. We hardly see you anymore." Laura puts a dish from the oven on the table and turns to her son to get a hug.

"It smells wonderful." She has made his favorite, grilled lamb chops with spinach and string beans.

Laura accepts the compliment with a hand gesture.

"Sit down, everything is getting cold."

Marc takes his seat across from his father. "Hi dad." It's been a month since they last talked in Isaac's office and Marc hasn't seen him since. Marc has been busy, and all their communication has been over email or phone.

"Good to see you, Marc." The old man doesn't look good. Age has suddenly caught up with him.

Marc is about to ask if he is well when his mom intervenes. "Tell me everything. What's new?" She brings a large bowl of salad to the table and joins them. Marc makes her laugh when he reminds her that when he was a kid he refused to eat if there was anything green on his plate.

They're having a nice meal together. *He should visit more often*, Marc thinks. His parents are not getting any younger.

"Can I help you with anything?" Marc asks his mom when she stands up to clear the dishes.

He knows better than to take any initiative in her kitchen kingdom.

"Just make yourself and Dad some Irish coffee. I'll take care of everything."

Irish coffee is the traditional Sunday dessert. Marc knows the drill. When he returns with the drinks, Isaac shifts the conversation.

"How are things in engineering?" Isaac can tell they are doing better because his phone is rather quiet, but he wants to hear more.

"We finished a lot of the projects that were close to completion and I expect that things will start moving faster now." Marc brings his father up to speed about the full-kit that is now mandated before they start working on a new project.

Isaac sees the full picture. "You could use a full-kit before production as well, so we no longer have incidents like the one we just had with the H355."

Marc is not surprised that his father knows about it. Somehow, he always knows what is going on. "Gate two is now in place," he confirms.

Isaac takes a minute to think. "We should also have gate three before integration."

Marc is amazed. He should have thought about it. This is

an important handover. When integration is getting ready to start working at a customer's site, they should make sure they've got everything they need from production, inventory, and engineering, as well as ensuring the customer is ready for them. This full-kit will save them a lot of grief and agony while ensuring faster and smoother installation at the customer's site. He'll talk with Roger, the head of integration, and bring him up to speed.

"Consider it done."

Marc contemplates sharing his own idea with his father. He should consult with him about it. Hopefully the old man will be willing to hear him out. Marc decides to go for it. "Actually, I wanted to talk with you about possibly adding gate zero."

"Gate zero?"

"Yes. At the very beginning, before we start working on the bids."

With smaller companies they conduct an analysis of the customer's needs, on or off-site and then submit a proposal, but with the larger customers they usually have to go through a bidding process.

"You know how we often have to chase the customers for missing details in the bid that are required for preparing our offers? Imagine how much time it will save us if we can get all the initial information in an organized manner. We can ask to work with them before they issue the bid to ensure all the needed requirements are..."

Isaac stops him right there. "Forget about it. These are our customers, Marc, not our employees! They have their own practices and it's not our place to dictate to them how to go about their business."

Marc is fully aware that they need to approach their large customers carefully with such an unorthodox suggestion. They should also be extra careful not to be accused of trying to rig the bids in their favor. But he can see that the customers have a lot to benefit from their help as well, if they could reduce the pain of going back and forth with multiple potential suppliers, answering questions regarding missing elements in the bids.

Isaac can tell Marc's idea has merit. On occasion, when they get to work on a new project, they find out that key details were missing from the bid and thus their estimate is off. Sometimes way off. In these cases, they either approach the customer to negotiate a later due date or a larger budget, or they bite the bullet and absorb the difference. Isaac can clearly see that having a full-kit for the bid would prevent a lot of these incidents. Nevertheless, it is out of the question. They are competing against much larger companies, which have more resources and flexibility to handle such issues. If they start dictating terms to submit the bids they will be out of the race before it even starts.

Marc tries to continue the discussion but his father refuses to listen.

Marc is dismayed. The concept of gate zero has merit. Enough to warrant a discussion of when and where it might be useful to have. Talking to his father was a bad move. He could have contacted one of their customers with whom they had a good relationship, perhaps one who had a similar incident lately, and gently explored the idea. But now that he has such a clear "no" from his father, he can't pursue it any further.

Bummer.

Marc has had enough. He gives his parents an excuse for having to leave, hugs his mother, and makes his way to the door.

Laura takes her time putting the leftovers in the fridge and filling the dishwasher.

Finally she says, "It seems to me that Marc had a valuable idea."

Isaac gets agitated. "He doesn't know what he's talking about. I have worked with these people for decades. I know how they think. They will not tolerate a supplier telling them what to do. Plus, they're under pressure to release the bids early and sometimes they don't have those details yet."

Laura closes the dishwasher and presses the ON button. "Isaac, you know your customers well, but so does Marc. I trust that he knows this is a delicate situation. That's why he came to consult with you. And you should trust him, too."

Isaac rejects the thought. "The kid is not ready. He won't make it."

Laura would have liked to ask why he believes he is the only one who can run the company, but she chooses her words carefully. "Maybe he will struggle a bit at first, but so did you. Why not give him a chance?"

Isaac sighs. "Back in the old days things were different. There was room for mistakes, which I admit I made plenty of. But now the competition is stronger than ever, the large companies rule, and more and more small companies like ours go out of business. There is no more room for mistakes."

Laura sighs. She is not happy with any of it. She is not happy that her husband is sick. She is not happy that he refuses to get treatment even if most probably it won't do any good. And she is not happy that he demands keeping it a secret from the kids. But he always respected her decisions, and she always respected his.

"I only wish you wouldn't risk your relationship with Marc," she finally says.

Isaac is determined. He has another meeting scheduled with Laramie's people. They want to move forward and he knows the drill with these large companies. Next they will ask him to sign a sixty-day no-shop clause, committing he will not solicit offers from other buyers while Laramie takes the time to do their due diligence. Isaac believes they are serious. He will sign.

19 ┃ Rework and Standardization

Rick enters the classroom and notices the word FO-CUS written on the whiteboard in giant letters. Probably a leftover from Johnny Fisher's previous class, "Production the T.O.C. Way." The eraser is nowhere to be found. Never mind, FOCUS suits his course just as well.[6]

He waits until everyone takes their seats and gets going. "A couple of weeks ago we had guests speaking about dosage. Any thoughts?"

Charlie says, "It's kind of a side note, but I was really impressed by how high up these managers are in their organizations."

"This side note is rather central." Rick plays on his words. "These organizational changes are so fundamental that they seldom work 'bottom-up,' only 'top-down'; you need some high-level managers to champion these changes, or better yet to lead them."

Charlie is relieved. "That's comforting to know. I have tried talking with my bosses about implementing triage and reducing the bad multitasking and I hit a brick wall."

One of his buddies says, "No worries, Professor Silver,

Charlie will find good use for this material. We all have bets on whether he'll climb up the ladder or end up having his own startup."

While Charlie is basking in his buddy's compliments, Rick moves on. "What else? What did you make of the shift from monitoring local efficiencies to overseeing the global flow?" he asks.

"I keep thinking about it," says Shonda. "It's a big shift in management attention. Not only does it provide a clear guideline for evaluating new procedures, it also helps sort the existing ones. So many of our efforts are directed toward improving local operations that have nothing to do with improving the flow. Getting rid of those local efforts will save us a lot of headaches."

Rick wants to make sure the students understand the difference between a local optimum and a global one. "We are used to thinking that if we find a way to become more efficient anywhere in our system, we should go for it. We assume that local efforts will add up and improve our overall performance. That is why we invest so much time, money, and resources on local improvements. But in fact, most of these local improvements are useless. A local change only makes a difference if it improves the overall flow."

Marc can see the ramifications. "These local efforts are not only useless, they are harmful. Our resources as managers are spread thin as it is, and when we spend them monitoring useless processes, we do it at the expense of investing where it matters."

"Precisely," Rick says. "Think about it, management attention is the number one constraint in most organizations. We better use it where it counts."

Rick knows that some people get this shift in perception right away and some people need to take their time. Either way, enough said about it for now.

Charlie is still pumped by his friend's endorsement. "Are there any other obstacles to flow we need to be aware of?"

"Well," Rick replies, "let's talk about an obstacle that you mentioned in our first class. Rework."

Charlie is allergic to rework. "Having to redo the same tasks is clearly a waste of time and resources, and by definition it unnecessarily clogs the flow."

Kiara can't help herself. She turns to her left and whispers to her colleague, "Speaking of rework, last night I was folding a mountain of laundry in the living room while the kids were playing on the carpet next to me. I was nearly done when I got a call and went in the other room for some quiet. I was only gone for a couple of minutes but when I came back there was not a shred of evidence that the laundry was ever folded. I had to start over."

"It could have been worse." Her colleague hides a smile and whispers back, "They could have eaten chocolate ice cream just before..."

Kiara laughs as quietly as she can. "It sure clogged the flow. Took me forever to refold everything, and I had so many other things to do."

Rick waits for the class to be quiet and continues. "If, on occasion, we have to redo something, it's not a big deal. But if there is an issue with the way we operate that makes us repeat certain tasks on an ongoing basis, it is definitely an obstacle to our flow that we should pinpoint and handle."

"What do you mean by 'pinpoint'?"

"What I mean is, rework doesn't just happen. We need to investigate what creates the need to redo the work, before we can figure out how to handle it. Charlie told us at the time that they suffer from rework because people above them keep changing the specs. We need to find out what causes these changes. Is it because they start to work too early before the scope of the project is finalized, is the goal of the project ill-defined, or is it something else?"

Rick pauses for a second, looking for a simple way to explain his next point. "Be aware that rework is an obstacle to flow on its own, but often it is a result of other obstacles."

"Can you give us an example of an obstacle that causes rework?" Marc asks.

"Sure. Awhile ago we talked about lack of full-kit. This major obstacle to flow often causes rework. For example, we have to get going on a task but we are missing a final decision from the customer. We make an assumption about what they will choose and just get started. Later we find out that our assumption was wrong and the customer wants something else and we have to start all over."

Marc sees what the professor means. "When rework is a result of lack of full-kit, then having a full-kit before we start will also eliminate the related rework."

Charlie can sense his allergy acting up. They already covered full-kit and he is not interested in repeating the discussion. "What other obstacles to flow cause rework?"

Rick is on board with moving forward. "Let's put rework aside for a minute and talk about another rule of flow: standard work. We often have places in our operation in which we tend to improvise. Some of us are masters at winging it, while others aren't. But, as a rule of thumb, improvising requires more effort and takes longer. If we improvise on a constant basis in important tasks, then it is most likely an obstacle to our flow."

Shonda the perfectionist adds, "When people improvise, especially when they work under pressure, they also tend to forget things, and the quality of their outcome suffers."

Rick agrees. "The way to improve the flow as well as the quality of the outcome, is to figure out what processes, or checklists, documentations, et cetera are needed to standardize the way we perform these important tasks."

Marc is thinking about the earliest stage in their process, when they write proposals. The argument with his father about gate zero still weighs on him, but there is more to it. What Professor Silver just said struck a chord—they do improvise on an ongoing basis. When they get started, they often open a new file and start from a blank page. Sometimes they sense that this is a waste of time, so they look for old proposals that they have written for similar projects and use one of them as a basis for the new proposal. Having a standard template is a simple solution. Marc likes the idea. If they come up with a standard format for proposals, it will be much faster than starting from a blank screen or looking for one of the old drafts. Actually, they can do much better. When they are working on projects that are using similar automation solutions, a large percentage of the project is the same and only a certain amount of customization is needed to tailor the robotic arms to the customer's specific needs. So they should have a few proposal templates that don't only contain titles. They should incorporate the general specs for their major types of projects and have blank spaces only for the needed customization. This is good! Having standard templates for their projects will significantly reduce the time it takes to write proposals.

Marc realizes that he hasn't been listening when he hears the professor answering someone.

"God forbid we just go ahead and standardize all our processes. In many places in our operation standardization won't impact the flow, so as we said, it's useless. In other places what we actually need is flexibility. Think about it, sometimes the true value of the project is actually in the nonstandard work; in the distinctive thinking and solutions that we tailor to it. Standard work is the rule to use only in spots where we recognize that improvising is an obstacle to our flow."

Rick continues, "Now, let's go back to our previous discussion about rework. I hope you can see that when we standardize the work, we also eliminate the rework created by improvising."

Marc sinks back into his thoughts. Once they receive a project, the assigned engineers usually start working on it from scratch. Marc is not used to thinking about it as rework, but in essence, it is. Considerable thought was already put into the project when they originally wrote the proposal, and now they are basically repeating the same work. Marc wonders why they do that. He figures it has to do with the fact that they are currently improvising. It seems it is often easier to start from scratch than to go through the agony of deciphering what was written in the proposal. Especially if someone else wrote it or if considerable time has passed since it was submitted to the customer. But if they start working with standard templates that everyone uses, it will make it much easier not only to write the proposals but also to use them as a basis for their work later. That would save time and further improve their flow.

Marc keeps thinking about standardizing the process of writing proposals. Who should be in charge of updating the templates and how to make sure this process is not forgotten after a while. When he turns his attention back to the class, he realizes that he has missed most of the lecture.

"We covered a lot today. We talked about the various aspects of rework and standard work," Rick starts to summarize. "I hope that by now you have a much better understanding of how to manage flow. There are different obstacles to flow, some are generic and we see them often, and some are relevant only to specific types of project environments. We will not be able to cover all the different obstacles in class, and we don't have to. I believe that by now you have enough intuition to identify when there is an obstacle to your flow and figure out how to overcome it by yourself."

Rick takes a breath and continues. "To practice, I'd like you to analyze, on your own, the aspects of synchronization. Synchronization is a rule of flow that is used in many project environments. It is especially relevant when one of the tasks in the project is considerably larger or longer than any one of the other tasks. In order to manage the flow effectively, we need to use that task as our anchor and synchronize all the other tasks with it."

"For your homework, choose a project that has just such a prominent task in it and figure out the needed synchronization."

Ted makes a lame attempt to excuse himself. "There is no such task in our projects."

But Rick is not letting him off the hook. "Then think of other construction projects that do have them. For example, when building high-rises, the construction of the steel and concrete frames that hold the weight of the building definitely qualifies." Rick wants to end the discussion nicely. "Or choose another project that has nothing to do with your line of work. It's up to you."

20 | Synchronization

A little after eight on Thanksgiving morning, Marc arrives at his parents' house. He was looking for a project that needs synchronization for his homework in the Rules of Flow course and figures that Thanksgiving dinner is a perfect fit. Obviously, the roasted turkey is the major task that takes considerably longer than all the others in this project. But when he tried to write his report, he realized how little he knew about making that dinner. Marc's usual assignments for the holiday include bringing Aunt Miriam from her retirement home, and making the guests happy with cranberry-apple punch while his mother is putting the final touches on her delicious dishes. Usually when Laura is working her magic in the kitchen, everyone else needs to make themselves scarce. But this year Marc asked to be her sous-chef.

When Marc enters the kitchen, he is surprised to find his mother sitting at the table having coffee. The turkey is already in the oven.

"Good morning, dear. Why don't you pour yourself

some coffee and tell me more about this homework assignment?"

"I'd like to know more about how you organize Thanksgiving dinner around the turkey."

Laura is happy to oblige. "Well, this is a complicated project that needs to be carefully planned and meticulously executed."

Marc knows he is talking to the right person.

"There are going to be fourteen of us this year. Knowing that enables me to calculate how many pounds of turkey we need and figure out the quantities for all the other dishes," Laura continues.

"You start by defining the scope of the project." Marc smiles. "I like your approach."

"Earlier in the week I made a comprehensive grocery list and double-checked that I got all the ingredients I need. If I find that something is missing in the middle of cooking, all my planning might go down the drain."

Here is the full-kit, Marc thinks to himself. "Tell me more about your planning."

"I calculate how many hours the turkey needs to be in the oven and that is the basis for the entire cooking plan. Since we sit at the table at three and the turkey has to sit for an hour after it is out of the oven, it had to go in before eight."

"That's really early!" Marc is surprised. "What about the stuffing?"

"Everything has to be carefully coordinated. To get the turkey in the oven by eight I needed to make the stuffing the day before."

Laura stands up. "Time to get back to work. Marc, why

don't you set the table?"

Marc goes into the dining room and starts to assemble the table extensions so the table can fit fourteen people. The regular members of the family are coming, as well as Sophia and her son and a few more people from work. People shouldn't be alone on Thanksgiving and everyone should be in a good mood. To avoid another quarrel Marc decides to stay away from his father. He will arrange to sit at the other end of the table. Marc gets the folding chairs from the basement and sets the table with the elegant china his mother loves.

When he comes back to the kitchen after a while, his mother is busy next to the stove. Trying to make himself useful, he gets the peas out of the freezer.

"Put the peas back, Marc." His mother doesn't miss a thing. "If we make the peas too early, they will get cold and mushy and we'll have to make new ones."

Poor synchronization can also create rework, Marc notes to himself.

"Why don't you come over here and peel the sweet potatoes." She points to the small mountain of sweet potatoes on the countertop.

"Sure," Marc says. "What happens now?"

"Well, since we only have one oven, and it is occupied by the turkey for most of the day, all the other dishes have to be planned around it. The sweet potatoes, white potatoes, and roasted vegetables have to be ready to go in the oven as soon as the turkey is out. Everything else was either made yesterday or will be made on the stove top."

"What about the green bean casserole?"

"We don't have space for it in the oven, so I make it in

the slow cooker, which I set for low temperature, so the cooking takes about four to five hours."

"You can cook it on high. It's way more efficient; you can get the casserole done in half the time."

"Now why would I want to do that?" Laura rejects the idea. "Who cares if I'm efficient in making the casserole? A couple of hours before we sit down I'm super busy with a bunch of other things and having to deal with the casserole at that point in time will mess things up. You need to look at the big picture, Marc. Take all the other tasks into consideration and see where would be the right time to take care of each dish."

Marc realizes what just happened. He was thinking in terms of local optimum: suggesting a way to use the slow cooker more efficiently. But his mother was right, of course. Thinking in terms of local optimum would mess up the synchronization. What matters is the global optimum: synchronizing all the tasks smoothly to get everything ready in time.

He looks around and asks, "What about the cranberry sauce? Are you going to make it now?"

"No. There is no time to make the cranberry sauce today. That's why I made it yesterday. It's already in the fridge."

Marc gets the picture. While peeling the sweet potatoes he tries to organize his thoughts about what he has learned. *To meet the due date on projects of this type, we have to start by scheduling the major task and then coordinating all the other tasks with it. We need to take into account how long it takes to perform each of the other tasks and what resources are required for them. We don't want to work on one task when we should be working on another, and we certainly*

*don't want to get stuck because we need a specific resource
while it is occupied by other tasks. Therefore, in the planning
stage we determine the right order of performing the tasks,
keeping in mind that some need to be completed before we
start working on the major task and which tasks can be done
in parallel. On top of that, we need to keep an eye out to ensure we don't end up with rework.*

Marc starts to appreciate what the professor meant when
he said that synchronization is an important rule of flow in
such projects. If anything goes wrong, they will either miss
some of the dishes (compromise on the scope) or have to
delay dinner (miss the due date).

Around noon Marc excuses himself and goes to get Aunt
Miriam. Aunt Miriam is eighty-five years old but sharp as a
tack. She lives in a home not too far from his parents' house.

While waiting to join the traffic on Main Street, his
thoughts go back to the concept of synchronization. He
is quite satisfied with his analysis. Although now that he
thinks about it, the synchronization in organizations is not
only between tasks. It's often between teams, or as in his
department, between people. Everyone in the department
is busy and each person has his or her own schedule and
priorities. Even arranging a meeting is often not a simple
task. It stands to reason that these synchronizations should
be done the same way that synchronization between tasks is
done. You need to identify the "turkeys", the key people who
are usually also the busiest, and synchronize everyone else's
schedules with theirs.

Marc pulls into the flow of traffic and keeps thinking. His
mother is synchronizing the tasks in one project, cooking

the Thanksgiving dinner. But what if it was a multi-project environment and she was also preparing a different meal for the neighbors? Things would get more complicated. The oven or the slow cooker might become an issue. If one or more of the dishes from the neighbors' meal needed to go into the oven while the turkey was in there, the neighbors' project would get delayed. The same goes if one of the dishes has to go into the slow cooker while the green been casserole is in it. In proper planning, in addition to synchronizing the tasks in each of the meals, there's a need to stagger the tasks waiting to be handled by the critical resources. Having a resource with limited capacity in the operation has to be taken into account in the planning stage, as it will inevitably effect a project's lead time.

Marc knows this issue is not unique to engineering. He can easily think of other project environments that do have critical resources, such as specialized testing labs, wind tunnels, and cranes. Marc arrives at the home and stops at the entrance to the main lobby. Aunt Miriam is ready to go. He helps her get into his SUV, folds her walker and places it in the back. As he gets behind the wheel, he braces himself for the unavoidable. Aunt Miriam has been asking him the same question since he was in high school, and Aunt Miriam never fails to deliver.

"Well, child, did you find yourself a nice girl?"

21 | One-on-One

It is Tuesday of the following week. It has been about a month and a half since they froze the projects and about a month since they started preparing full-kits. Linda will be in his office in a minute for her one-on-one.

Marc has a weekly one-on-one with each of his project managers. He tries to limit them to ten or fifteen minutes each, so they take less than a couple of hours a week. Time well spent. He cares about his people and wants to know they are doing well. He also cares about their work; if something distracts them or if they are stuck, he prefers to know about it sooner rather than later.

The routine is well known. Marc asks how they are doing, making sure "their world is round." He tries to find a mutual interest they can briefly chat about on an ongoing basis. Then he wants to know about their projects. He can tell these short meetings make a difference and his people look forward to them. They like their personal time with Marc when it's about them and no one else.

Marc maintains a running dialogue with Linda about the best places to go out. Linda has a nose for them. Today she recommends a new brasserie downtown.

"You have to check it out. The decor is really cool, and the food is to die for."

"Sounds like my kind of place."

They move on to talk about work. Linda brings him up to speed on the code she is working on for one of their cutting edge projects. By using AI capabilities they are able to make the robotic arm adjust its reactions to changing conditions in ways that weren't possible before.

Linda is their expert in the most advanced software and is also their go-to whenever there is a problem the other software engineers can't handle. She is one of the busier people in the engineering department, if not the busiest.

Marc knows some people have been complaining and he wants to know what's going on. "How is it going with reducing the multitasking?"

"It sure helps that we are working on less projects at a time," Linda is happy to report. "But I also made some changes on my end. Before, my day was full of constant interruptions. Anyone who encountered a problem with the code would request my immediate attention and I kept bouncing between projects. Now I'm trying something else. No one is allowed to interrupt me when I'm working. Whoever needs my help can alert me on the collaboration tool. Every few hours when I finish a task, I review my alerts and if something is high priority I take care of it before moving to my next task."

Marc totally agrees. "That way you keep an eye on everyone, you don't hold back important projects, and you get a lot more done."

Linda can tell that avoiding the bad multitasking makes her work much more efficient, but it is harder than she thought. "People don't like it that I'm not available to help whenever they need me. It may take them awhile to get used to the new situation and stop pressuring me to multitask."

Taking into account people's impatience and their need to make progress in their own work, Marc believes she may always need to fight the pressure to multitask.

Linda definitely intends to continue with her new routine, but it does come at a price. "In a way, it isolates me from the rest of the group. It helps that I can talk with you about it."

Marc knows what Linda is talking about. Sometimes it gets lonely being the manager or the expert. He assures Linda she can always come to him for support. As for himself, he used to have his father to talk with, but lately it's not the case.

"Anything else I can help you with?" Marc asks.

"Actually, yes."

Linda says that being the software expert takes so much of her time that she can hardly pay attention to the project she is in charge of and consequently they are running late on it.

"I would like to dedicate all my time to software."

Marc realizes once again how his perception has changed since he started thinking in terms of flow. Being a small company, traditionally all their senior engineers became project managers, with no exceptions. But now he is thinking that if Linda has to multitask between her responsibilities as their software expert and managing her own projects, one has to come at the expense of the other. Looking at the big picture it makes sense for Linda to work solely on code. He grants Linda's wish and makes a note to put her project on hold and as soon as possible assign it to someone else.

It's dark outside when Marc leaves the office, but he doesn't feel like going home. He has spent too many evenings alone in his apartment lately. He decides to go downtown and check out the new place that Linda recommended.

When he enters the restaurant, he notices someone familiar having a glass of wine at the bar.

"Hi Abbie."

"Fancy seeing you here, Marc." Abbie seems happy to see him.

"Linda told me about this place."

"Yeah, she said I had to check it out."

Abbie invites him to join her and they order dinner. The conversation drifts naturally from work to other subjects and they are both pleasantly surprised when they find out how much they have in common. Dinner is over but neither of them seems in any particular hurry to call it a night.

22 | What Changes Should We Expect?

Before Rick opens the lecture, Shonda raises her hand. "Professor Silver, I have a question."

"Go ahead."

"Let's say that we implement the rules of flow that are relevant to our environment, what changes should we expect? What will be different?"

"Good question and good timing; we'll get to that later today. But first there is another element in the way you currently do things that we need to discuss."

Rick begins by setting the stage. "Working on projects involves considerable risk management; uncertainty is pretty much the name of the game."

People are nodding their heads. Rick continues, "We are all aware of the uncertainty. Since every project is different, we can't really tell how long it will take to complete it. Tasks may take longer than planned and unexpected delays may occur. That's why people end up putting so much safety into their time estimates."

"So much safety?" asks a familiar voice from the corner. Ted plays right into Rick's hands. "Let me ask you, Ted, when one of your site managers asks his crew how long it is going to take them to complete a certain task, do they give him or her an estimate that reflects the time it will take them to perform the task if everything goes smoothly?"

"They're not stupid," Ted replies. "They know better than that. They've been whacked over the head for being late before, and they'll do whatever they can to avoid it. They'll give a much higher estimate; an estimate that they believe they can meet even if something goes wrong."

"So, they are in fact putting safety into their estimate, right?"

Rick keeps pressing, "And what about the time estimates that the roofers give, and the plumbers and the electricians? They all know that things tend to take longer than planned. They all give your site manager time estimates that are far from the minimum and already contain a lot of safety, isn't that true?"

Ted is reluctant to admit to anything.

Shonda is familiar with the situation. "You're right. Only a newbie will give a time estimate that doesn't contain safety, and after the first time they are late and penalized for it, they'll learn their lesson and never repeat that mistake again."

Rick continues. "There's a lot of safety imbedded in the task level, but not only there. What happens when the site managers need to give their time estimate to headquarters? Will they simply sum up all the estimates they received from the people on the ground and forward this number?"

"Probably not," Shonda says. "They suffered the consequences of their people being late more than once and to protect themselves, they'll add their own safety."

"Correct, and what happens at headquarters before they commit to the customer? The person in touch with the customer is the one who gets the criticism firsthand every time they are running late, so he or she is bound to add their own safety to the overall time estimate."

"Hold on." Marc has to interrupt. "We still have to make sure that the final due date we give the customers is in the ballpark of what they expect, or we won't get the project to begin with. So whoever is in charge often has to cut back the final time estimate that they get from their people."

"Excellent." Rick is pleased. "This is the dynamic of how time estimates are made, in most project areas. The bottom line is that even if some of the safety is cut at the end, as Marc said, we still have plenty of safety imbedded in our time estimates."

Ted doesn't buy it. "If there is so much safety, then how come we don't see many projects finish ahead of time?"

"That's because you're doing a very good job wasting it," says Rick.

Shonda speaks for everyone when she asks what he means.

"First and foremost, the obstacles to flow use up the safety. If you don't control WIP, the constant multitasking between projects and between tasks can eat all of it. Remember we said that multitasking is the biggest killer of time in projects? The same goes if you keep having to stop and wait for things because you don't consistently have a full-kit or if you don't synchronize tasks when you should, et cetera."

"Okay, we covered the obstacles to flow," Charlie says. "Is there anything else that wastes the safety?"

Rick confirms that there is. "Take for example the student syndrome."

He notices the puzzled looks and smiles. "Let me ask you something. Weeks ago, when I gave you the homework about full-kit, you claimed that a couple of weeks was not enough and insisted on getting more time. I doubled your lead time and gave you four weeks to complete the assignment. How many of you went home and started to work on it right away?"

Now everyone smiles. As expected, many of them had waited until the last minute to start working on the homework and a couple of them missed the due date and had to ask for additional time.

"I see what you mean," Kiara says. "Student syndrome happens everywhere. We are wasting the safety before we even start working on the project. No wonder that we often have to rush to finish on time, or we deliver late."

"I have to say that I did start right away," Shonda says, "and I didn't finish ahead of time. I kept thinking of more people to interview to ensure I had full-kits and come up with better ways to monitor compliance, and I literally finished just because I ran out of time."

"What you are describing is a classic example of another phenomenon that wastes safety: Parkinson's Law."[7] Rick recites, "The work expands so as to fill the time available for its completion. We keep embellishing our work, adding features and polishing the results until our time is up."

"That's me all right." Shonda grins.

Rick continues, "There are also other cases in which people finish their tasks early, but they are reluctant to report it. They are concerned that if they disclose that they didn't use all the time they were given, next time management will not trust their time estimate and will cut it. And next time things may not go as smoothly, and they may very well need the extra time. So, if they are done early, they keep quiet and report the completion of their task on its due date."

"Smart people," Ted comments.

Rick concludes, "In most projects we put a lot of safety into our time estimates. At the same time, instead of using this safety wisely, we end up wasting it. So, more often than not we end up rushing to finish projects on time."

The class is quiet. People are thinking.

Rick moves on. "Now I get to your question from the beginning of the lecture, Shonda. What happens when we start controlling WIP and removing the other obstacles to our flow?"

Marc recalls how hectic things used to be not so long ago. Everyone was busy trying to get things done but not much was accomplished, and it was hard to tell what was causing the constant delays. All that had changed once he started controlling WIP. Once he limited the number of projects his people work on in parallel, the chaos went away, and they were able to really focus on the few projects they were working on. Soon after, the need for full-kit surfaced, and once they took care of that, they started to move faster. Rick wants to help the students put the pieces of the puzzle together. "Before, you put in a lot of safety and you wasted it, resulting in long lead times and frequent tardiness.

Once you remove the major obstacles, the main thing that happens is that the flow of projects gets going. The work is getting tighter. There is no use for most of the safety that is imbedded in the time estimates and you will be able to finish the projects much earlier than originally estimated."

The work is getting tighter. The students are trying to visualize it.

"Let's see what that means." Rick opens his bag and digs out a marker. He draws a series of rectangles on the whiteboard.

"Here is a simple project with four tasks. Once we've removed the obstacles to flow, you'd expect it to go from start to finish smoothly." Rick adds arrows going in one direction. "But in fact, people still get stuck every now and then."

"Stuck?" Charlie is alarmed.

"It's not like unicorns appear out of nowhere and hold people from doing their job. It's ordinary things that are keeping them from moving forward today. For example, they run into an issue that they need an expert's help to resolve, or they need something that requires a manager's approval."

"Right. We do get stuck a lot." Charlie has no shortage of examples. "Like, a week ago my team found a problem that could be easily fixed by another team. We asked our manager if we could transfer the task to them or spend a lot more time working on it from our end." He chuckles. "As a matter of fact, we're still waiting for her to decide."

Rick adds a large rectangle above the project's tasks and writes "experts/management" in it. Then he adds arrows going up and down from the project's tasks to the large rectangle. "This is what the progress of the projects looks like."

The Dynamics of a Project

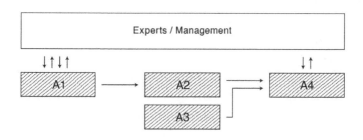

Being one of the top experts in her IT division, Kiara knows well what it entails. "The experts and/or the managers have to address whatever it is that people need as soon as possible, in order not to hold them back and enable them to continue with their work."

"Correct," Rick agrees. "Taking into account that this is one of several projects that run in parallel and all of them need the experts/management attention from time to time, the experts and/or managers have their hands more than full."

In fact it is now clear that they are the system's constraints. The resources with the most limited capacity relative to the demand. But not everyone is familiar with the concept of constraints. Rick decides to focus. He'll get to it later. "In order for the work to get tight we have to avoid delays. The experts and managers need to be as efficient as possible and do their best not to hold the projects back.

Solving problems should become one of their top priorities."

Marc exhales. Making problem-solving a top priority is easier said than done. There is just not enough time in the day. His thoughts circle back to the status report meetings. A lot of their time is tied up in them. Too much. There has to be a way to simplify how they monitor the progress of the projects.

Marc forces himself to concentrate when he hears the professor is moving on.

"The managers and the experts need to make the commitment to help the work get tight, but they can't do it alone. Everyone should be encouraged to bring up problems as soon as they surface so that they can be addressed as early as possible."

Charlie says, "If we bring up problems we'll be hushed up. So we keep quiet for as long as possible."

Rick explains. "If you have a task that should take ten days and you wait until the eighth or ninth day to alert your manager that something is wrong, most probably you won't finish the task on time. But if you alert the manager on the first or second day and it's a high priority for them to help you, there is a much better chance the problem will be resolved without a delay in the project."

Charlie has his doubts. "That's very different from the way things are today. They would have to completely change their attitude if they want to encourage us to come to them early."

"You bet it's different," Rick emphasizes. "It is a real cultural change. We promote a culture of flow; of fast-moving projects. It requires trust between management and the people in the trenches. Management should be available to solve problems as soon as they arise, but everyone will have to change their behavior. People will have to get used to focusing on single tasks and avoiding multitasking. They have to adhere to preparing full-kits. They have to alert someone as soon as problems arise and pass the baton as soon as they are done. We let go of the hidden safety in the projects so there is no tolerance for unnecessary delays. There is no more room for student syndrome or Parkinson's Law. We are all in it together, with collaboration and good will."

This is a lot to take in. Adopting these behaviors is at the heart of maintaining a fast-moving flow. They continue to discuss the various aspects of this cultural change until the time is up. Rick wishes them a good winter break and dismisses the class.

While Marc is gathering his stuff, he overhears Kiara and her colleagues talking next to him. They are wondering how the experts can manage to address everyone's problems in a timely manner. But something else is bothering him. Marc leaves the classroom and walks to the cafeteria to get coffee before his next class. He can't shake the feeling that something is missing, but he can't put his finger on it.

23 | Taking Precautions

It's after breakfast on New Year's Day. Marc is at his sister's house in the Southeast. He had flown in the day before to spend the holiday with his sister and her family. The weather is cloudy and chilly but nothing like the bitter cold at home. Marc is eager to spend some time outside. Dave had suggested the two of them go biking. Dave and his father, Jack, are keen cyclists. They have plenty of gear and Marc is about the same size as his brother-in-law. Jack gladly offers him one of his road bikes and proper clothing.

While Dave makes sure they have everything they need, Marc rides in circles in the driveway, getting used to the bike and reacquainting himself with using clip-in pedals. It has been awhile since the last time he rode, but he quickly recalls how to latch and release the cleats.

Dave comes outside with his hands full. He places a couple bottles of water in the special holders secured to each bike and fills the pockets in the backs of their shirts.

Sam appears at the door. "Dinner is at six. And I want you sitting at the table showered and nicely dressed!"

Marc salutes. "Yes, ma'am!"

"No worries, Mom." Dave knows what his mother is concerned about. "We'll be home before it gets dark."
Sam goes back into the house as Dave puts on his helmet and gloves.

Marc asks, "What time does it get dark?"

"After five."

"I want us to be home by three," Marc says.

"That's fine by me." Dave knows the perfect route.

They get on the bikes and start pedaling through the streets on the way out of town. Marc follows Dave closely, watching the sparse traffic and getting used to balancing himself on the bicycle. After a while he relaxes and starts to enjoy the floating feeling of cycling on a high-quality carbon bike. Soon they are out of town and onto the country roads. It's clear that Dave knows where he is going; he has been on that road many times. The clouds begin to part, the sun appears, and the asphalt is dry. A perfect day for a bike ride.

They ride past open fields and oak and pine groves. It's beautiful here in the summer when everything is green, but even now it has its charm. Marc has a sensation of freedom he hasn't felt in a long time. He switches gears and accelerates, unbothered by the wind on his face.

Dave reaches him after a little while. "You might want to pace yourself."

Marc is on a roll. "Don't worry. I can handle it."

Dave feels responsible. Marc is making a mistake. He is obviously in good shape, but strength training does not require the same kind of effort as cycling for several hours.

He needs to find a way to explain this to his uncle.

"Hey Marc, slow down. I want to ask you something."
Reluctantly, Marc slows down. "What's up?"

"Why did you tell me earlier that you want to be home by three o'clock?"

Marc wonders what made Dave ask. "I wanted to make sure that we get home well before dark. Unforeseen delays can always happen, so I included a buffer."

"Buffer?"

Marc takes a deep breath. "A buffer is a specific type of precaution. You add more to what you originally estimated in case something unexpected happens and you end up needing it. In our case, we had six or seven hours of daylight, so I asked you to choose a route of four to five hours and left a couple of hours as a buffer. That way, if we have a flat tire or something, we will still be back before it gets dark."

"I see," says Dave. "You took a time buffer to protect us against unexpected delays."

"That's right."

"That's a pretty large buffer. What if I suggest that in addition to the planned route, we turn left at the next intersection and add a scenic road that will take us an extra hour?" That's why Dave had asked him to slow down.

"That sounds great," Marc replies, "but maybe another time." He trusts Dave but he is still the adult here. What if Dave's estimate is off and the ride takes longer? What if they make a wrong turn and it takes awhile before they realize it? He should explain this to Dave. "If we use up half the buffer right at the beginning, and something goes wrong later, we may not have enough time. We risk having to ride in the dark. It's better to save the buffer for the end of the ride, not

139

spend it at the beginning."

"That makes sense," Dave says. Marc's response was exactly what he had hoped it would be.

Marc is getting ready to accelerate again when Dave continues. "You know, Marc, on the bike you are the energy source."

"So?"

"If you run out of energy, you're in trouble. So, in addition to time, there is something else that we need to watch today, and that's our energy."

The kid is right.

They cannot afford to run out of power. They need to take a buffer of energy in case they need it later.

"Point well taken," Marc says in admiration. "Thanks for slowing me down. It's not wise to spend all my energy at the beginning."

"Better save it 'til the end." Dave is relieved. "If we get to the last part of the route and you still feel you have a lot in you, knock yourself out."

They keep going. Every once in a while, they pass by a classic barn, a small picturesque church, or a country store with old gas pumps. After an hour or so they stop for a break. Marc pulls a couple of energy bars out of one of his pockets and hands one to Dave. He swallows his bar in a few bites and pulls out another one.

"Marc, wait," Dave says. "All the food we have for the ride is what's in our pockets. I doubt any of the convenience stores in the gas stations are open today or have vending machines that actually work."

Marc pauses, impressed. "You sure know how to keep

an eye on buffers."

"Every cyclist does." Dave is proud of the compliment. "I didn't know how much food you'd need, so I brought more than I would normally take. But we still have to watch how much we eat."

"How do you usually go about it?"

"We eat enough to maintain our energy. We can't afford to run out of power, but we don't want to eat too much, either. We also monitor the amount of food we have left relative to how long we still need to ride. Hopefully we'll arrive home with some left over. But if we see that we're running out of food, we'll have to do something about it, depending on how long we still have to go."

The hours go by and Marc and Dave have a great time. They get back shortly before three. Marc is exhilarated and tired at the same time.

Dave had done a good job monitoring their breaks and food intake. He gave Marc most of the energy bars and gels he brought, and even mixed electrolyte powder in Marc's water when they filled their bottles at one of the churches along the way.

But after close to five hours of biking, Marc has to admit he has no energy left. He has to sit down for a while before hitting the shower. They certainly did the right thing taking the time buffer, energy buffer, and food buffer. Moreover, they kept an eye on how they were doing on these buffers in relation to how long they still needed to ride.

When something important is at stake, you better have buffers.

Something important. Marc's thoughts wander to the

engineering department. Making sure they deliver the projects on time is highly important. It finally dawns on Marc what he was missing in Professor's Silver's last class. Once they started to implement the rules of flow, the work got tight; they let go of a lot of the safety. But unexpected delays are bound to happen, and they have no buffers.

24 Buffer Management

Rick arrives to class feeling a bit nostalgic. Back in the days when he first started teaching project management according to the Theory of Constraints, the concept he was about to cover took up a large portion of the course, but a lot has changed since then.

He decides to start slowly. "Projects vary in how important it is to meet their due date. On one end of the scale, there are projects that have a rather vague due date, like some academic research or art projects. On the other end of this scale there are projects for which meeting the due dates is of the utmost importance."

Rick pauses briefly to let the students think where their projects are on this scale. "If your due dates are not set in stone, then most likely removing the obstacles to your projects' flow is all you need to focus on. But," Rick raises his index finger to emphasize what he is about to say next, "if meeting the due dates is key in your line of work, then in addition to managing the flow you also need to take precautions to ensure you meet your deadlines."

"What do you mean by taking precautions?" asks Charlie.

"Well, just like money that you set aside in case you have some unforeseen expenses, you set aside time buffers in case you have some unforeseen delays."

Bingo. Marc is relieved. This is what he had been looking for. In everyday life Marc has no problem figuring how much of a time buffer he needs, but when it comes to managing the projects in engineering, he hopes the professor can give him some pointers. "How do I determine how much time I need to set aside?"

"Good question." Rick turns to the whiteboard and writes "Buffer Management" in large letters.

"A good rule of thumb is to take a third of your estimated time for the project and use it as your buffer."

"A third?" Shonda asks. "So, if I estimate that a certain marketing project will take three months I should attempt to finish it in two and keep one month as a buffer? That's very tight."

"When removing the obstacles to flow the work will get tight," Rick reminds her. "And if you have any unexpected delays...you have a whole month buffer to use."

"Where would I take that one month from?" Shonda is still hesitant.

"To get started it would be best if your projects are planned in a way that is easy to monitor. For a two-month project you'd like the length of your tasks to be around a week each. For a two-year project each task should take around a month."

Everyone is quiet. Rick proceeds. "Let's take a simple three-month project as an example. As we said, we'll divide it into tasks that each take about a week." Rick turns to the whiteboard and draws a row of twelve rectangles. "Now, simply cut one third from the estimated time for every task and place all that time as a buffer at the end of the project."

Buffer Management – The One Third Rule of Thumb

1	2	3	4	5	6	7	8	9	10	11	12

1	2	3	4	5	6	7	8	9	10	11	12	Buffer

Rick draws another line of twelve thinner rectangles and adds one last rectangle that takes up about a third of the line. He writes the word buffer in it while saying, "Always place the time buffer at the end to protect the whole project."

Rick turns to face the class and continues. "What I suggest is that you get together with your teams and discuss their time estimates for each task. You may need to ask a few questions but sooner or later they'll tell you that their estimates consist of the actual time they think it will take them to perform their task, plus safety they believe they need to guard against issues that may come up. They don't invent these issues. They are guarding themselves against things that happened in the past and caused them significant delays, so pay attention."

They have already discussed the excess safety that people hide in their tasks' time estimates, so everyone is on the same page.

"Okay, and then what?" Marc asks.

"Explain to them that from now on you will be keeping the safety time for everyone and that is why you are cutting their estimated times by a third. Give them your word that if what they are concerned about happens, they should come to you and you'll grant them the extra time they need."

Marc wants to make sure he understands. "So, instead of each team holding on to their own concealed time buffers, I should keep one overt buffer for everyone."

"Correct."

Marc thinks about the rule of thumb the professor just described. On one hand, the buffer should be large enough to make his people feel they are protected against unexpected delays. On the other hand, the buffer should not be so large as to promote Parkinson's Law and the student syndrome. One third sounds about right.

Rick wishes to show them the whole picture. "Once the project gets going, whenever one of the teams is in need of more time, you grant it to them, push the next tasks forward and deduct that time from the buffer. If you see that too much of the buffer was consumed and you are not close to completion of the project, you may need to take corrective actions, like assigning more people to the project, using outside vendors, et cetera to speed things up and ensure that you meet the deadline. On those occasions where there is nothing you can do to rectify the situation, at least you can alert the customer ahead of time to expect a delay."

"Hold on," Marc says. "Can you explain more fully what you should do when people use up the buffers?"

"Of course." Rick prepares himself for a long explanation. "When people approach their manager asking for more time, the first thing the manager should do is grant them the time they asked for. That's the right thing to do for the project and that's also the right thing to maintain people's trust that if they need additional time they will get it."

That's important, Marc is thinking. *If the manager won't give them the time, it pretty much guarantees that people will start concealing safety in their time estimates again and the flow will go to hell.*

Rick goes on. "But a wise manager will not stop there. You need to distinguish between genuine uncertainty and wasting buffers. Unexpected delays will occur, we know that, that's why we keep buffers. And if people ask for more time because something unexpected happened, that's fine. But if they are asking because the time was somehow wasted, you need to be aware of that and see to it that it doesn't happen again."

Rick takes a breath and continues. "Start your inquiry by asking when they found out they would need more time. If they found out about it early on they should have alerted you then, when the delay might have been avoided. People have to get used to alerting management as soon as the problems occur. They have to get used to the behaviors that support the flow, and it's the manager's responsibility to hold them accountable if they don't. The same goes if you find out that the delay occurred because people were multitasking or they neglected to prepare a full-kit, et cetera."

Kiara says, "So, after we grant the time people asked for, we need to look into what caused the delay, and if we find out that people did not adhere to the expected behaviors they should be held accountable for it. What else should we look for?"

"Well, one of the things that managers often find, especially at the beginning, is that the same issue causes delays in various projects. That means they need to consider resolving this issue ahead of time."

Kiara completes the professor's sentence. "So they should add it to the full-kit."

That's a good option, Marc thinks. He keeps an eye out for things that should be added to the full-kit with his WIP board. But many organizations don't use WIP boards, or they only use them to monitor tasks, the way Abbie does. It's a good idea for managers to learn if things are missing from the full-kit by analyzing the consumption of the buffers.

"Another thing that managers sometimes find," Rick continues, "is a person or other resource that is busy to the extent that queues of work start to pile up in front of them. These cases should also be resolved and there are various ways to go about it."

Marc recalls the one-on-one with Linda when she told him about her effort to manage her time as efficiently as possible. She was also right to ask to be excused from certain duties that could be carried out by other people.

Rick summarizes. "By keeping a close eye on the buffers and holding people accountable to the right behaviors, managers make sure that time is not wasted and the fast flow is maintained."

Shonda wants more details. "How exactly do I keep a close eye on the buffer?"

Rick replies, "You monitor the progress of the project in relation to the buffer."

"Let me show you." Rick finds an empty space on the

whiteboard and draws a chart that shows the percentage of project progress vs. the percentage of buffer consumption.

Project Status Chart (A Fever Chart)

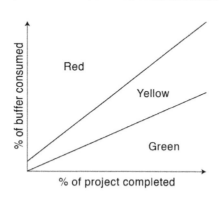

He explains, "This is a project status chart, or a 'fever chart,' as we sometimes call it. As you can see, as long as you complete a larger percent of the project relative to the percentage of buffer you consume, you're in the green and everything is fine. When you start to consume a larger percent of the buffer you get into the yellow. You need to be aware that you might use up the entire buffer before you complete the project, which means you might be late. That's why when you're in the yellow it's time to make contingency plans. Figure out how to rectify the situation if you keep having more delays. And if you happen to get into the red, then there is a real risk you'll be late. It's time to put the contingency plans that you came up with into action."

Shonda says, "Okay, this is helpful. Although I have to say I'd prefer to monitor the consumption of the buffer myself, not just passively wait for people to come to me and ask for more time."

"By all means," Rick agrees. "Every day you should ask the people working on a given task how many days they need in order to complete it. If they have five more days in the plan and they say they'll be done in five days, then everything is fine. But if they say something came up and now they need eight days to complete their task, you know it will use up three days of the buffer."

"I see," says Shonda. "You monitor the consumption of the buffers by getting daily 'remaining duration updates.'"

Rick wants the class to have a better sense of the scale. "For a three-month project I'd go with daily duration updates. But if the project is scheduled to take two years, it is sufficient to get the remaining duration updates once a week."

Before the students ask more questions, Rick wants to summarize. "We start by ensuring that our project is planned in reasonably sized tasks. Then we use the one-third rule of thumb to establish the buffer."

Everyone is taking notes. "Once the project gets going, we monitor the consumption of the buffer closely, by receiving daily or weekly remaining duration updates. Whenever someone approaches us asking for additional time, we grant it to them but we look into what caused the delay and respond in accordance to what we find out."

Rick concludes, "As the project progresses, expect that some delays will happen and a portion of the buffer will be consumed. That's the nature of projects. As long as the time left in the buffer is reasonable relative to how close the project is to completion, it's fine. But if the buffer is eaten up to the point that you start to worry it might jeopardize the due date, take corrective actions. You don't have to invent anything. You take the same corrective actions you take today when you are concerned you'll be late. Only with buffers you'll have to resort to these means a lot less often and probably much earlier."

Rick pauses for a minute and then adds in a firm voice, "A word of caution. If you don't properly control your WIP, don't bother with monitoring the buffers—you will consume them for sure. The same goes if you keep having to stop and wait for things because you don't consistently have a full-kit or if you don't synchronize tasks or resources when you should, and so on. Managing the flow will get you to shorten your lead time and meet the other projects' requirements. Watching the buffers is only the mechanism to ensure you are on track to finish on time."

═══

The lecture is over and people leave the class. Marc approaches the professor and asks if he has a minute.

"Why don't you walk with me to my next class?" Rick grabs his bag and heads to the door.

"Sure."

As they walk down the corridor Marc explains the situation. "My projects take about three months but they consist of so many little details that often take less than a day."

Rick is familiar with the situation. "How did you end up monitoring your projects on such a detailed level?"

Marc needs a minute to recall. "When someone messes up in a way that causes a considerable delay, we dig deeper and look into what caused the delay in the project. We ended up adding more and more details to our status reports to make sure we don't overlook them again. Over time we went into finer and finer detail and by now the lists we cover in our status reports are rather long."

"So, what I'm hearing you say is that you check the status of all these details to ensure accountability and basically to protect yourself against delays. Can you think of another way to achieve that?"

Marc stops walking. The buffer management they just discussed is by far a better way to guard against delays. If he switches to monitoring his projects in larger one-week tasks, all his project managers have to do daily is ask for remaining duration updates. That will take minutes instead of going line by line over the long lists of status reports.

Letting go of checking the status of these many details shouldn't be taken lightly. He has been relying on these status reports to hold his people accountable for as long as he can remember. But does he really need them anymore? Most of the screwups were a result of the chaos they operated in, but now that they are avoiding a lot of the bad multitasking and having full-kits, people can concentrate and they make fewer mistakes. Most of these details don't really need to be monitored anymore, and he can think of other means to check the ones that do. He had been hoping to find a way to shorten the time the status report meetings take, but now it seems like he can let go of these meetings altogether. The project managers can use the time to solve problems. Hell, they can use the time to make progress on the projects!

Marc thanks the professor and continues to his next class, wondering how his people will react to this radical change. He smiles to himself. After the past few months they were used to his unorthodox ideas. *It'll be fine.*

25 | Lead Time is Getting Shorter

The weeks go by. January is almost over. Marc can tell that the lead time of the projects is getting considerably shorter. Most of the nineteen projects they kept in WIP were completed and by now they are working on the projects that were originally frozen. The lead time varies of course, so he is thinking in averages, but it seems that the remaining time for the completion of projects was cut by about half. Marc contemplates when the right time to talk with his father will be. He has been avoiding his father since their argument about gate zero. He didn't want his father to stop any more of his initiatives, and to his relief, his father didn't make much effort to talk with him, either. But they should talk soon. Marc only wants to wait for a few more projects to be delivered so the results cannot be disputed. They should start planning how to capitalize on the shorter lead times. Even with buffers, their promised due dates are significantly shorter than everyone else in the industry. Not only are they getting out of the ditch, the potential for growth is amazing. They can enter more bids, perhaps larger ones they had always avoided in the past. They can expand and open another location. Heck, they can open a few more. They can buy other struggling robotic companies and turn them around.

They can...

His cellphone rings. Marc doesn't recognize the number. The voice on the other end says, "Hello, am I speaking with Mr. Wilson?"

"This is he."

"I'm calling from Paul Becker's office. We'd like to arrange a meeting for next week. Will Thursday at ten work for you?"

The name doesn't ring a bell. "I'm sorry, who?"

The man on the other end of the line sounds surprised. "Mr. Becker is VP of finance at Laramie."

An alarm goes off in Marc's head. His father had mentioned he was talking with Laramie about potentially selling them the company, but that was over three months ago and he hasn't heard anything about it since.

"Can you tell me what this is about?"

Marc can hear the man talking with someone in the background. "It's about the purchase of your company, sir. We have completed our due diligence. We would like to meet to close the deal. The no-shop term is about to expire."

Marc is astounded. His father is selling the company behind his back. He can't believe that he's hearing about it by chance just because the buyer's assistant, or whoever he was, called the wrong Wilson.

"Let me check my schedule and call you back," Marc mutters, and hangs up.

Marc hurries over to his father's office. The door is

closed, but he doesn't care if he interrupts his father in the middle of a meeting.

As he is passing Sophia, she says, "He's not here. He took the day off."

"He...what?" His father hasn't taken a day off for as long as he can remember.

"Actually, he wasn't here yesterday either."

That figures, there's no reason for him to come in if he's selling the company. Marc thanks Sophia and calls his father's cellphone as he heads back to his office.

It takes a few rings before Isaac answers. "Yes, Marc."

"We need to talk."

"Yes, we do. Come over to our house for dinner on Saturday."

"It can't wait."

"Saturday, Marc," says his father and the line goes dead.

Marc is beside himself. He can't possibly get any work done. He stands in his office staring out the window. The clouds are thick and grey.

Yes, his father told him he was looking for a buyer, but he didn't say a word about signing anything. Marc is getting angrier and angrier. They hadn't lost a single customer since Doolen. Marc worked his butt off to improve the operation, and for what? For nothing. At the very least his father owed him the courtesy of keeping him in the loop. What a messed-up situation, and for no reason. The numbers may not fully reflect it yet, but they are doing better than they have done in a long time.

Abbie pops her head in the door. She can tell something is off. "Is everything okay?"

Marc can't stand staying in the office for one more minute. He has to get out of there.

"Will you go for a drive with me?"

Abbie wonders what's going on. It's not like Marc to leave the office in the middle of the day. "Okay. Let me grab my coat."

They take off in Marc's SUV. The snow on the ground is a few days old and is mixed with dirt. Marc keeps his eyes on the road as he drives over patches of ice and puddles of slush. He's heading out of town.

Abbie sits next to Marc quietly, giving him time. He'll talk when he's ready.

After a while Marc says, "I need to tell you something and I need you to promise not to say a word about it to anyone."

"Okay."

"My father is selling the company."

"What?!" Abbie is stunned. "Why? We always assumed you would take over when he retires. And why now, when we're turning things around? What am I missing?"

Marc looks at Abbie briefly and then moves his eyes back to the road. "I'm wondering the same thing myself."

"What do you mean? What did he tell you?"

Marc tells her how he found out. "One thing is for sure, I'm not staying. I'm not working for them even if they ask me to stay."

Abbie starts to wonder if she needs to worry about her job. Probably not, and she'll think about it later. Right now she feels as if she needs to be there for Marc.

"I understand why you wanted to get out of the office." She puts her hand on his shoulder to console him. Then she sheepishly takes her hand back.

They drive quietly for over an hour. It's getting dark. Abbie is relaxed, looking out the window. Marc can feel his tension slowly starting to fade. He looks at Abbie, hoping she won't notice. She is beautiful. It feels nice to be in the car with her.

They enter another town.

"Would you like to stop somewhere?" he asks.

"Yeah, it'll be good to stretch our legs."

They approach the center of town. The well-designed street lights are on, adding to the pleasant atmosphere. Marc finds an empty space. He pulls over and they get out of the SUV. It's freezing outside. They walk for a little while. Marc can tell Abbie is cold. He puts his arm around her to keep her warm.

Is it appropriate? He couldn't care less.

Abbie gets closer to him. She turns to face him and looks up. Marc lifts his other arm to hug her closer. Their eyes lock. The kiss is exactly as he had imagined.

Back in the SUV Abbie looks at Marc and says, "You know we can't. We work together."

Marc comes back to reality. "Not for long."

26 | How to Get Started

Early on Saturday morning, Marc is in a terrible mood, just going through the motions at the gym. He needs to pass the time until meeting his father. He doesn't feel like going anywhere but he can't stand the thought of counting the hours at his apartment. He might as well go to the university.

"For your final assignment," Rick opens the lecture and gets right down to business, "I'd like you to conduct a full analysis of implementing the rules of flow in your multi-project environment."

Everyone gets talking, asking questions, pleading, and arguing. It happens every year. Rick is not flustered. They don't know how to get started.

To help calm things down Rick says, "We all want the same thing. We want to go from a reality where we have frequent delays, things take forever and we are constantly multitasking, to a reality where the lead times are much shorter and the chaos goes away. Let's discuss how to facilitate this transformation."

Finally the room is quiet. "You know that if you don't cut the WIP, the multitasking will continue, causing the delays and long lead times. So, one way or another you'll have to cut the WIP. To do that, you first need to be clear on what units you use to describe your WIP. What sort of projects or elements of projects are you multitasking between? Marc, you use the terms 'projects' or 'development projects,' and Kiara, you talk in units of 'work packages.'"

Charlie says, "We only have one project in our company, and that's the software we're developing. We are multitasking between 'features.'"

Rick turns to Ted. "You said that your company has fourteen construction projects and that's a given. So to cut the WIP, obviously you won't freeze construction sites. I wonder what you call the 'units of completion' or 'throughput units' when you're describing progress toward completing the construction. Remember, we don't care about the productivity of a single worker, we ask what are the units that need to move faster in order to improve the flow of the whole system."

Ted doesn't answer. He is too busy thinking how to evade the colossal assignment that just landed on them.

Never mind. Rick figures the students get the idea. "Once you determine the throughput units your people are multitasking between, you can contemplate how to cut them in the WIP. Following what we discussed in class, there are a few strategies to consider. The most prevalent strategy is the one that Marc used. Freeze a large percent of the projects and keep the ones that are close to completion, or the ones with the highest priority, in the WIP. The multitasking goes down significantly and you keep controlling WIP as you go.

When one project is completed a new one enters the WIP."

Shonda asks, "What if freezing projects leaves some people with nothing to do until their project is back in the WIP?"

"Everyone should take part in getting the flow going. No one stands on the sidelines. If they cannot assist in other projects, assign them to help with full-kitting."

There are no other questions, so Rick moves on. "In internal projects, such as IT departments, you'll probably consider a different strategy: triage. By identifying the projects with low value and canceling them, you practically achieve the same objective: you reduce the number of projects in your WIP.

Kiara says, "I'd like to add something if I may. We found out that triage is not only about canceling work packages with low value. We also came up with new high-value ideas that should have top priority."

"That's interesting. Can you give us an example?"

"Sure," Kiara says. "When we were going over the long lists of work packages in our WIP we realized that we were literally maintaining four generations of the bank's software. Every few years we introduced new software but we kept maintaining the previous one, mainly as backup but also because some features worked better in the older version. Supporting four platforms is a huge effort that takes up a lot of resources and budget. So, we made it a top priority to ensure that the new software is up to par and we can discontinue all its previous generations. Once this is done it will reduce our WIP considerably."

"Excellent idea!" Rick praises Kiara and continues. "We covered two strategies to reduce WIP, let's move on the third one. In project environments where there is a massive amount of integration and people are constantly stuck because things are missing, it makes sense to start with full-kit. Construction is a classic example for such an environment, so it's no surprise that Ted's ears perked up when we got to it in class. In this strategy you continue to work only where you have a full-kit and everything else is placed on hold, which also means you cut the WIP. You prepare the missing elements for the full-kits and gradually bring the project back into the WIP.

Charlie says, "To get the flow to move faster, I would guess that Ted would also like to end up with less construction projects in WIP. So it stands to reason that he prioritize the order in which he brings the fully-kitted units back into the WIP in a way that facilitates completion of projects."

"You bet." Rick is glad to hear them starting to develop the intuition for flow.

He goes on. "The fourth strategy that I'd like to mention is relevant to project environments that suffer from bad outcomes where people have to fix the same problems again and again. In these cases, dosage is likely the preferred strategy to control WIP."

"Okay," Shonda says, "we choose the most relevant strategy to our operation and we cut the WIP. What happens next?"

Rick smiles. "Remember how soon after Marc froze half of his projects the need for full-kit surfaced? That's how it works every time. The multitasking creates such turbulence in the flow that it's really hard to see past it. But as soon as you cut the WIP and the multitasking goes down, the flow becomes clear. We can see what other obstacles need to be removed and what else needs to be taken care of. Just keep your eyes open and pay attention to the progress of your projects. I can tell you that often there is a need to change the roles and responsibilities of some key people, and of course if you have to protect your due dates, place suitable buffers and monitor them closely."

Marc has been following along rather halfheartedly until now, but there's something he wants to know. "Can we go back to cutting the WIP for a minute?" he asks. "How do we know how many projects we should have in our WIP?"

Rick has been waiting for that question. It's time someone brought it up. "Remember that we discussed what changes when the work is getting tight?"

"Yes," Marc says, "you drew that illustration of the people needing assistance from the managers and experts every time they run into a problem they can't solve on their own."

"Right," Rick says. "The managers and experts are usually the most precious resource in the operation and are also the most scarce. Which means that they are the ones who are in most demand. They are the constraints, the resources with the least capacity in the system."

"So?" someone asks.

"So, what happens if the managers or the experts can't handle all the issues that need their attention in a timely manner?" Rick retorts with a question.

Kiara knows. "Queues will start piling up in front of them and people will have to wait. It will slow the flow down."

"And what does that tell you?" Rick presses on.

Marc sees where the professor is going. "That may indicate there are too many projects in WIP."

"Correct. There is no point in having long lists of issues waiting in line for the managers and experts to resolve. The number of projects that they can effectively handle is the number of projects we should have in our WIP."

"I see." Kiara gets the picture. "If these experts have time on their hands we can add more projects to the WIP, but if lots of problems start piling up for them to resolve, we know we hit the WIP limit."

"For now treat it as your WIP limit and make the effort to find the other obstacles you need to remove and the other changes you need to make to get the flow going. In a rather short amount of time you'll complete a bunch of projects that were in their last stages, and by then things will start to settle down. You will get used to controlling WIP, preparing full-kits, et cetera, on an ongoing basis."

Some people are nodding their heads, some are still thinking.

Shonda says, "Moving forward, there will be pressure to increase the number of projects in the WIP."

Rick agrees. "To increase the capacity of your system you'll have to focus on the constraints. First, identify these few people who are in fact your system's constraint. Then figure how to exploit the constraint—how to make the best use of their time."

Shonda says, "These are usually the most responsive people, the ones who are more than willing to help. They take a lot on their shoulders. There has to be a way for them to delegate at least some of their responsibilities."

"That's definitely the way to start," Rick agrees, "but there is more to it. These experts have the most experience and intuition. Right now they are preoccupied with fighting fires and solving problems in the projects that are already late or are close to it. Moving forward, these experts should get more and more involved in the earlier stages of the projects. That way they can anticipate a lot of the problems and prevent them."

Marc understands. "The experts should be involved in full-kitting the projects."

"The more they are involved in full-kitting," Rick explains, "the fewer problems will occur down the road. Which means they will spend a lot less time firefighting and you can add more projects to your WIP."

Rick doesn't stop there. "At this point if you are short-handed, you can find more people to run your projects. These people are easier to find and less costly then the experts."

"Finding more experts is close to impossible," Kiara says.

"You don't have to go outside to find them," Rick replies. "Your experts will be devoting a large percentage of their time to analyzing upcoming projects and full-kitting them. Get good people to help them. That will not only make the experts' work more efficient, it's the best way to grow your next experts from within."

Marc can't help but think: *What a great opportunity this is to grow. For companies who are serious about it, who have the discipline to follow through and the confidence to endure this amazing cultural change, even the sky is not the limit.* Too bad he is not going to be able to implement it in the family company. Selling it at this point in time is such a shame.

The students ask some more questions about their final

assignment. Rick knows it is a lot of work. To alleviate the pressure he says, "You'll have the rest of the school year to work on it."

The students exhale in relief and Rick adds, "To overcome student syndrome, next class I'll pick one of you to present their initial analysis."

27 | The Contingency Plan

Marc approaches his parents' house. There is a rental car parked in the driveway. Sam is probably there. It figures, his father wants to tell both of them the news about selling the company. That's why he didn't want to talk with him on the phone. Marc feels his anger growing again. That is what his father would consider fair.

Marc enters the house and notices the wonderful smells coming from the kitchen. Before he can take his coat off, his niece jumps on him with a hug. "It's about time. We were waiting for you."

"What are you doing here?"

"Grandpa said we should come so we got on a plane and came. He's talking with Mom in the study."

Marc heads to the study, feeling knots in his stomach.

"Come in, Marc." Isaac doesn't look well.

"Did you know about this?" Sam is snapping as soon as she sees Marc. "Did you know that Dad is sick?!"

"Dad is what?"

"He is seriously ill. And he didn't bother to tell us, or do anything else about it."

"Dear, I know you're upset, but I'm telling you now," Isaac says quietly and turns to Marc. "Sorry I couldn't talk with you the other day. I was in the hospital and the doctor had just come in to tell me they want to admit me for further testing. I wanted to know where I stand before we talked." Isaac continues to explain what the doctors said.

"What do you mean there is no treatment?" Sam is adamant. "You have to fight no matter what!"

Isaac is gentle but firm. "I have made my peace with the fact that I'm sick. There is nothing that I can do about it. But I still have a little time, and what I do with it is my choice."

Marc is dumbfounded. When he realizes he is still standing, he sits down, not saying a word.

"What about Mom?" Sam asks.

"You know I love your mother very much and she is well taken care of. What I'd like to do now is quit working and spend the time I have left with her."

"What about the company?" Sam keeps asking.

"You made up your mind a long time ago, Sam," Isaac reminds her. "And as you wished, you will receive your share, but will not be involved in any management decisions."

That was her choice. Having her father coaching her to manage the company would mean she would have to stay close and follow his directions, and she didn't care for that. She needs to be in control. "I'm going to check on Mom."

Isaac turns to Marc. "It is for a reason that I stayed away lately, son. I wanted to give you space to try this new way of running things."

Marc finally finds his voice. "It works well. At least hear

me out, let me tell you about it."

Isaac continues, "I know. Although I gave you space, I kept a close eye on things and I'm very impressed by the changes that you made in such a short amount of time. It's still early, but it is clear that you are on to a much better way of managing our projects."

Isaac raises his hand, gesturing to Marc he has more to say. "When you got started, I wasn't at all sure that you were going to pull it off. In fact, your mother had to remind me that I should trust your intuition. You need to know that back then I made a contingency plan. Laramie is interested in buying us. You should be hearing from them soon because the no-shop clause I signed is about to end. In full disclosure, I told them that you are making some significant changes in engineering that could affect the final numbers. They just let me know they completed their due diligence and I gave them your number. The company is yours now. I'm here to help, but whether you sell or keep the company is your choice."

Marc grins. "Well, I wonder what they'll say when they hear that the changes in engineering affect not only the numbers, but the nature of the deal. I'm not looking for a buyer, I'm looking for an investor."

Rules of Flow

- Avoid bad multitasking, control your WIP

- If you don't want to get stuck, verify full-kit before you get going

- Triage to ensure you are working on the right priorities

- Ensure synchronization between your tasks/people/ resources

- If you keep going back to the same projects and you don't get the desired results, look into the option to increase the dosage

- Avoid unnecessary rework by finding what causes it

- Standardization is recommended when improvising is costly

- Abolish local optimum, global optimum is what matters

References

1   Goldratt, Eliyahu M., Cox, Jeff, *The Goal: A Process of Ongoing Improvement*, 30th Anniversary edition, North River Press, 2014.

2   Goldratt, Eliyahu M., *Critical Chain*, North River Press, 1997.

3   This article was originally published in the December 2008 issue of Diamond Weekly, Japan. It was added to *The Goal* in the 30th Anniversary edition.
Goldratt, Eliyahu M., "Standing on the Shoulders of Giants." In Goldratt, Eliyahu M., Cox, Jeff, *The Goal: A Process of Ongoing Improvement*, 30th Anniversary edition, North River Press, 2014.

4   Goldratt, Eliyahu M., Goldratt-Ashlag, Efrat. *The Choice*, Revised Edition. North River Press, 2010.

5   Little's Law in projects: Throuput X Lead Time = WIP,
Little's Law (2021, October) In Wikipedia. https://en.wikipedia.org/wiki/Little%27s_law.

6   Focus is the main concept of the Theory of Constraints.
Goldratt, Eliyahu M., Introduction to T.O.C.—My Perspective. In Cox, J. F., Schleier, J.G., *Theory of Constraints Handbook*, McGraw Hill, 2010.

7   Parkinson's Law is a well-known phenomenon that should be taken into account in project environments.
Parkinson, Cyril Northcote, "Parkinson's Law." *The Economist*, 1955.
Fowler, Elizabeth M., "It's a 'Law' now: Payrolls grow." *The New York Times*, 1957.

Other Goldratt books published by Routledge

The Goal
The Goal: A Business Graphic Novel
It's Not Luck
Critical Chain
The Choice
Isn't it Obvious?